CONTENTS

MARCO POLO

PRAGUE

with Local Tips
*The author's special recommendations are
highlighted in yellow throughout this guide*

There are five symbols to help you find your way around this guide:

Marco Polo's top recommendations – the best in each category

sites with a scenic view

where the local people meet

where young people get together

(100/A1)
pages and coordinates for the street atlas
(O) *outside area covered by the street atlas*

MARCO ⊕ POLO

Travel guides and language guides in this series:

Algarve • Amsterdam • Australia • Berlin • Brittany • California
Channel Islands • Costa Brava/Barcelona • Costa del Sol/Granada
Côte d'Azur • Crete • Cuba • Cyprus • Eastern USA • Florence • Florida
Gran Canaria • Greek Islands/Aegean • Ibiza • Ireland • Istanbul • Lanzarote
London • Mallorca • Malta • New York • New Zealand • Normandy • Paris
Prague • Rhodes • Rome • Scotland • South Africa • Southwestern USA
Tenerife • Turkish Coast • Tuscany • Venice • Western Canada

French • German • Italian • Spanish

*Marco Polo would be very interested to hear your
comments and suggestions. Please write to:*

North America:
Marco Polo North America
70 Bloor Street East
Oshawa, Ontario, Canada
(B) 905-436-2525

United Kingdom:
World Leisure Marketing Ltd
Marco Polo Guides
Newmarket Drive
Derby DE24 8NW

*Our authors have done their research very carefully, but should any errors or omissions
have occurred, the publisher cannot be held responsible for any injury, damage
or inconvenience suffered due to incorrect information in this guide*

Cover photograph: Charles Bridge, Castle (Mauritius: Mehlig)
*Photographs: HB-Verlag, Hamburg (7, 8, 78, 95); Janfot (17, 29, 62, 70); Kallabis (32, 44,
53, 55, 60, 69, 87); Mauritius: Enzinger (82), Hubatka (12, 18), Lawrence (4),
Ley (99), MacLaren (47, 76, 81), Rawi (48), Torino (30, 64), Witzgall (38)*

2nd revised edition 1999
© Mairs Geographischer Verlag, Ostfildern, Germany
Author: Lubor Vorel
Translation: Andrew Bredenkamp, Lawrence Brazier
English edition 1999: Gaia Text
Editorial director: Ferdinand Ranft
Chief editor: Marion Zorn
*Cartography Street Atlas: © ADAC Verlag, Munich; Haupka Verlag, Bad Soden;
Mairs Geographischer Verlag, Ostfildern*
Design and layout: Thienhaus/Wippermann
Printed in Germany

Discover Prague

The royal and imperial city invites you to visit its historic buildings and squares, see its art treasures, and enjoy its Bohemian cuisine

'The stones on the bed of the Vltava constantly move. Three emperors lie buried in Prague. The great do not remain great, and small not the small. The night has twelve hours, and then comes the day.' Bertolt Brecht wrote those words in his famous *Song of the Vltava* in the dark year of 1943. In his poem, Brecht sings the praises of the time of change in which Prague was the fabulous royal and imperial city.

Prague is one of the most beautiful cities in the world. Most people probably know the massive Hradschin with the Imperial Castle high over the Vltava which flows beneath the Gothic arches of the Charles Bridge. Next to Athens, Rome, Paris and London, Prague is one of the most historic cities in the West. No other city has as many epithets attached to it: the Golden City; the City of a Hundred Towers; the Symphony of Stone, Colour and Shape; the City of Legends; the City of the Golem, of Kafka, of Schwejk. Kings and emperors summoned the best architects in Europe to their courts to build magnificent religious and secular buildings. In an area of just 800 hectares, more than 2000 important buildings were erected, among them about 70 noble palaces, 80 churches and 35 monasteries. These, including the famous Strahov Monastery, were restored in recent years to the Catholic Church.

Prague has been home to three different peoples: the Czechs, the Germans and the Jews. This cohabitation, defined by peaceful competitiveness but also through productive and sometimes sharp discord, gave rise to much that was culturally and economically spectacular.

The Second World War, however, saw one ethnic group almost made extinct, and another driven away. The Czechs had little time to be at ease before the dark historical night

The Gothic Church was the centre of the Hussite religious reformers

Czech Wine

It is said that the Hungarian King Ludwig had barrels of wine placed in the streets for the people 650 years ago when making what was supposedly a courtesy visit to Prague. By the next day Prague had succumbed to the wine, and the Hungarians took the city. To give his people some practice in dealing with this insidious weapon, Charles IV brought in vines from Burgundy hidden in honey barrels, thus signalising the start of viticulture in Bohemia and Moravia. One still sees today in the many wine cellars how seriously the people of Prague foster their powers of defence. Suppliers of these high-quality weapons are the wine growers from sunny southern Moravia. The best white wines, Ryzlinka Rýnský and Vlašský, or the Pálava wine, come from Znojmo, Velké Pavlovice and Mikulov. In Bohemia the Lobkovicz princes are responsible for the good quality of the red wines from Roudnice, or the white wines from Mělník. One can sample the grape juice from southern Moravia everywhere, the Lobkovicz wines only in the princes' own wine taverns.

came that Brecht speaks of. From the East came a new dictatorship lasting some 40 years, during which the Stalinist regime exercised unrelenting control over the lives of the Czech people. 'The great do not remain great', Brecht had prophesied.

In November 1989 students, artists and ordinary citizens awoke to a new dawn. Like Sleeping Beauty after the prince's kiss, the dormant beauty of Prague began to awaken. The city rubbed the sleep from its eyes and slowly restored itself to its former splendour. The famous sites, which had been closed for decades, were then opened to the public. The delightful Royal Gardens, with the large ballroom, the gardens of Prague Castle, Vrtba Garden, the terraced gardens on the south side of the castle hill, and the stately Gothic Charles Hall in the Old Royal Palace are now accessible. The famous Triforium Gallery in St Vitus Cathedral, with its 21 remarkably life-like busts (1374–1385), is finally open again for all to admire. Concerts now take place in the gigantic garden of Prague's first Baroque palace, in which the musicians sit in the magnificent Sala terrena. The palace was named after its architect Valdštejn (the enigmatic Wallenstein), and was the seat of the Ministry of Culture, which the people of Prague dubbed the 'Anti-culture Ministry' during the totalitarian regime. The Foreign Ministry is now in the colossal Černín Palace. In 1948, shortly after the communist coup, the Foreign Minister Jan Masaryk was found dead beneath one of the windows. All the evidence pointed to another, the 'Third Prague Defenestration.'

Although it will be a long time before the country recovers fully from the economic, ecological and moral problems caused by the communist regime, the people of Prague have already begun to shed their sad and resigned expressions. This cautious optimism is reflected in the sinking rate of suicide: from 2820 deaths in 1970 to 1568 in 1996.

What is the true character of the people of Prague? In the 1960s, Prague-born German writer Johannes Urzidil wrote: 'The Czechs were long considered a warlike and aggressive people, lively and full of initiative, particularly when they were able to rely on natural or elected leaders; but we have also seen long intervals of passive, sad resignation, inter-spersed with flashes of uprising and rebellion. This duality is plainly visible in the music, art and literature of the Czech people.' In this light, Václav Havel is perhaps the ideal leader of the new Czech Republic.

The peaceful November Revolution of 1989 brought a significant change to people's lives. The inhabitants of Prague often refer to events as occurring 'before or after the November.' Before November 1989 political jokes were commonplace; they are now rare. The irony previously used as a defence mechanism against the hardship of everyday life under the communist regime is no longer necessary. Likewise Schwejkism, aimed at attacking the stupidity of violent authority, is no longer relevant in this new democracy. The

Music, architecture and a park: the Sala Terrena at Waldstein Palace

people of Prague know that it is time for engagement, energy and initiative. But there has still been problems: redundancy may be low but the inflation rate is still as high as ten per cent.

The inhabitants of the capital get up early in the morning. Although restaurant prices have risen, the locals still goes out to eat – if they can find a table not occupied by foreign visitors. On the one hand, the locals grumble, but on the other they are happy that the foreigners are interested in Prague. The city now attracts more tourists than Venice or Florence. This invasion occasionally annoys the inhabitants of Prague; they love their city and their River Vltava and are often angry over the polluted air and dirty streets. At weekends, however, they load up

their cars and drive off to their *Chata* (a weekend house) or *Chalupa* (an old farmhouse), happy to leave the city to the foreigners for a couple of days. At the weekends one meets almost only tourists in Prague – in the *U Fleků* with its 30 proof beer, in the *U Tomáše* with its black beer, or in the *U kalicha* with its 12 proof *Pilsner* beer. Most of the visitors to these central watering holes are German, while the Italians flock to the bars of the Little Quarter to savour the wines from South Moravia. And the Japanese, as always, are to be found behind a camera. The most popular international rendezvous has for some time been the picturesque Golden Lane which is almost too narrow to cope with the profusion of visitors.

With all the buskers, singers and hawkers, the magnificent

Old Jewish cemetery: stones laid as a memorial on the graves

Prague Cobblestones

Many of the pavements in Prague are decorated with mosaics of coloured marble, and the roads are mostly cobbled. The cobblestones, however, have greatly deteriorated over the past 40 years for lack of proper maintenance. The drive through the bumpy city is called the 'Prague Rally' by sardonic locals.

Charles Bridge is not wide enough to accommodate the flocks of people from all over the world who have come to admire the Baroque statues that decorate this wonderful open-air museum. Legend has it that wine and egg shells donated by all the Bohemian parishes were added to strengthen the mortar when the bridge was built – perhaps it is the only reason it does not collapse under the weight of so much human traffic. There may actually be some truth in the legend since recent studies have revealed that the mortar does in fact contain organic material. Six hundred years on, the locals still joke that the wily citizens of Velvary brought their eggs hard-boiled.

Pride and interest in their history is a characteristic of the people of Prague. Their castle is not just the former residence of kings and emperors. Hradčany is a symbol of their independence and autonomy that dates back over 1000 years to the reign of Prince Wenceslas, who was later canonised and became the patron saint of the Czech people. The Czechs have chanted ever since their moving anthem: 'Holy Václav, Duke of Bohemia, preserve us and our children!' It was not by coincidence that the biggest demonstrations during the 'Velvet Revolution' of 1989 were centred around the statue of the prince, seated majestically astride his steed, that dominates Wenceslas Square. This square, which actually resembles a broad boulevard, has been dubbed by tourists the 'stomach of Prague' due to its profusion of restaurants, bistros, cafeterias and wine bars. Together with the streets Na příkopě, Ulice 28. října and Národní třída, it forms the so-called Zlatý kříž – the Golden Cross. This is a favourite haunt of Prague's young folk, who gather around the café terraces 'by the horse' (the Wenceslas statue). Numerous banks and jewellery shops are to be found here now. At the hotels you will often encounter groups of visitors sporting name tags identifying them as participants in one of the many international conferences. Prague is again becoming one of the most important political and cultural centres of Europe. One can often hear it said that Prague is returning to Europe. Prague is also attracting increasing numbers of business people and entrepreneurs who have high hopes for the ever improving economic situation. Called 'the Paris of the twenties and the thirties' for its flair and cultural attractions, the city on the Vltava has attracted around 60,000 foreign residents in recent years, including thousands from America, Britain, Germany and the Netherlands, who now run various firms, bistros or cafés. Unfortunately, the Mafia has also infiltrated the city. 'The little mother has claws', wrote Franz Kafka. Hector Berlioz had 'a tender longing for Prague and its inhabitants', and Richard Wagner called Prague 'the unforgettable city'.

Princess Libuše, the founder of Prague, stood above the Vltava at Vyšehrad and prophesied, 'I see a great city, the glory of which will reach to the stars.' Twice in its history Prague has ranked among the most famous cities in Europe, and both times the glory ended in catastrophe. The heyday of the country under Charles IV was followed by the destructive fury of the Hussite Wars, and the prosperous reign of Rudolf II was followed by the Thirty Years War. In both cases a 'defenestration' marked the beginning of the tragedies. 'Prague is tragic', was the opinion of the French historian Ernest Denis.

'The stones on the bed of the Vltava constantly move', wrote Bertold Brecht poetically, and the history of the city on the Vltava is constantly moving. The history begins with the legendary Princess Libuše, the great mother of the Přemyslid dynasty which ruled Bohemia continuously from the 9th to the 14th centuries. The country was Christianised during

the reign of the famous prince, later to become Saint Wenceslas (907-935), and under Otakar II it developed into a major power. The 'Iron King' was defeated and killed in 1278 by Rudolf von Habsburg, the scion of the dynasty, and was to prove a very significant event in the history of Bohemia. Prague basked in a golden age under Charles IV (1346-1378), the son of John the Blind of Luxembourg (1310-1346) and Eliška (Elizabeth), the last Přemyslid princess. He built the Charles Bridge, several Gothic churches, and in 1348 founded the first central European university and the New Town. During the reign of his son, Wenzel IV, the economic crisis of neighbouring countries extended to Bohemia, and the impoverishment of the people led to the growth of radical movements opposed to the wealthy church. The first European reformer, Jan Hus, was burnt at the stake in Constance as a heretic. In 1419 the Hussites threw a number of Catholic councillors from the windows of the New Town hall. This 'First Defenestration' marked the beginning of the Hussite Wars (1419-1436).

With the marriage of Ferdinand I in 1526, the first Habsburgs came to the Bohemian throne. Rudolf II settled in 1526 in Bohemia, which was quite wealthy at the time, and made Prague his imperial residence. Prague under Rudolf became the glittering centre of the empire, and astronomers, artists and alchemists flocked to the city from all over Europe. But the discord increased between the Protestant majority and the Catholic minority supported by the Habsburgs. After the death of Rudolf II, the Habsburgs moved to Vienna, and the Bohemian Protestant aristocracy threw the remaining Habsburg governors from the windows of Prague Castle in 1618 (the 'Second Defenestration'). At the beginning of the Thirty Years War, the famous Battle of White Mountain was lost by the Protestants, whereupon some 150,000 men, among them the intellectual élite of the country, left their homeland. The last shot in the Thirty Years War was fired in 1648 in Prague during the siege by the Swedes. The country was then ruled for a further 300 years by foreigners and the Habsburgs. The subsequent return to Catholicism is connected with the construction of the majestic Baroque buildings.

In the 19th century, a growing national pride led to a rebirth of the Czech people and the founding in 1918 of the Czechoslovakian Republic. In the 1938 Munich Treaty the Republic was handed over to Nazi Germany.

The Communists came to power through a coup in 1948, and in 1968 Alexander Dubček attempted to reform the totalitarian state. Soviet tanks finally brought this budding 'Prague Spring' to a violent end. The first demonstrations of 1988 and the subsequent turn to democracy of 1989 finally put an end to the Communist regime. In 1993 the country was finally split into two independent states, the Czech and the Slovak Republics.

It is quite interesting to note that the years ending with the figure 'eight' have generally turned out to be fateful for the country. The question remains, what will the coming years bring? Can the country again blossom, and can the damage left by the totalitarian regimes be repaired?

We began with the words of a poet, and another voice should be added to that: 'I do not assume that the people, whose language I speak, are better or worse than others. I am at one with the fate of the world's catastrophes, and I have a little freedom, to live and to die.' (Vítězslav Nezval: *Prague and the Noon Sun*, written approximately 1930.)

In the spirit of Marco Polo

Marco Polo was the first true world traveller. He travelled with peaceful intentions forging links between the East and the West. His aim was to discover the world, and explore different cultures and environments without changing or disrupting them. He is an excellent role model for the 20th-century traveller. Wherever we travel we should show respect for other peoples and the natural world.

What shall we go to see?

A citizen of Prague guides you through the city with its monumental castle, gardens and squares, churches and palaces

Most visitors come to Prague for a short holiday. In three to six days, however, one can see only a few of the most important sights and attractions.

A good place to start a tour of Prague is on the Coronation Procession which leads from the Powder Tower to the Royal Castle. Stop off along the way to the castle and savour a glass of fine Moravian wine in one of the Vinárna (wine taverns) or drop into a Pivnice (pub) for a cold frothy beer. Take your time, sit back and look around, relax and absorb the atmosphere.

A city tour by bus is recommended to give you a general overview. The drive from one historical site to another will bring you unforgettable impressions. A more original way of seeing Prague is by taking a boat trip along the Vltava. It allows a panoramic view of the city and the magnificent buildings of the quays.

The imposing four-square Castle and the St Vitus Cathedral rise over the Charles Bridge

Prague, which was built on seven hills, presents itself best from the higher vantage points: from the Royal Palace ramp the entire city with its sea of towers and domes lies at your feet, and likewise from the tower of St Vitus Cathedral or the famous terrace restaurant 'The Golden Spring'. At noon the air reverberates with the sound of church bells that were banned for so long. The heavy echo of the Sigismund Bell, installed in St Vitus Cathedral in 1549, carries for miles, and the multitude of bell towers in the town below ring out their response – it is on these occasions that one senses how old and unique Prague actually is. The famous changing of the guard takes place at midday.

The charm and beauty of the capital on the Vltava can be admired from the top of Petřín Hill, where a miniature version of the Eiffel Tower, originally built for the 1891 Prague Exhibition, still stands. Other views can be enjoyed from Letná Hill, or looking down from the Old City or Little Quarter bridge towers, and from the Powder Tower.

13

Belvedere (101/F4)

The most beautiful Renaissance building this side of the Alps. A summer palace surrounded by fine arcades, it was built between 1538 and 1564 by Ferdinand I for his wife, Queen Anne, to designs by Paolo della Stella. The reliefs in the columned hall depict mythological hunting scenes and pictures of everyday life. Here one finds *Leda with the Swan* or a portrayal of the king offering his wife a flower. There is a wonderful view of the castle from the balcony. In the Renaissance garden stands the bronze *Singing Fountain* by Tomáš Jaros, which dates from 1564. If you crouch next to the bronze bowls at the base of the fountain, you can hear the musical sounds made by the falling water.

Only during exhibitions; daily except Mon., 10 am–6 pm; Mariánské hradby; Metro: Hradčanská (A)

Charles University (Karlova univerzita) (109/D2)

The oldest university in central Europe celebrated its 650th anniversary in 1998. Its founder Charles IV placed it under the protection of the patron saint of the Bohemian nation, St Wenceslas. Teaching in the four faculties took place in Latin, as was the rule in the Middle Ages. The university was accommodated in various monasteries until Wenceslas IV placed it in the notable house of the mint-master Johlin Rothlev in 1383. All that remains of the original Gothic house is an artistically significant oriel window of a former chapel and an arcade. The façade of the Carolinum was rebuilt in 1718 mostly in the

MARCO POLO SELECTION: SIGHTSEEING

1 Old Jewish Cemetery
Jewish cemetery of universal significance (page 20)

2 Astronomical Clock
The apostles parade on the Old Town Hall (page 18)

3 Castle
Monument of a thousand years. Triforium Gallery in St Vitus Cathedral (page 30)

4 Kampa
Romantic walks (page 27)

5 Charles Bridge
Open-air gallery of statues (page 19)

6 Loreto Shrine
Magnificent Diamond Monstrance (page 16)

7 Church of St Niklas
Symbol of the high Baroque in Prague (page 23)

8 Fred and Ginger
Original building by a US star architect (page 15)

9 Terrace Gardens
Prague Castle gardens (page 27)

10 Wenceslas Square
The lively heart of the city (page 30)

Baroque style by František Maximilian Kaňka. The heart of the university, the Great Hall, was created during this period, where Latin is spoken to this day at academic celebrations. On the end wall here hangs the tapestry depicting *Charles IV Kneeling Before St Wenceslas*, inspired by a silver seal dating from 1348. The Charles University has played an important role in the history of the nation, and the loss during the Second World War of Charles IV's Founding Charter, the precious Papal Charter and the valuable university insignia is still greatly mourned by all the Czechs. *Železná ulice; Metro: Muštek (A and B)*

Clementinum (108/B2)

After the Habsburg Ferdinand I had acquired the Kingdom of Bohemia through his wife (1526), he summoned the Jesuits to this overwhelmingly Protestant country. Between 1653 and 1727 they constructed, under the leadership of Francesco Caratti and František Maximilian Kaňka, the largest building complex, after the Castle, on a site of two hectare in the vicinity of the Charles Bridge, which was the spiritual stronghold of the Catholic Counter Reformation. It includes the Welsh Chapel, the churches of St Clemens and St Salvator, four inner courtyards and an observatory with a tower, its roof crowned with a statue of Atlas. Today it houses the National Library with more than five million volumes and about 5000 medieval manuscripts. *Entrance Křižovnická, Karlova ulice, nám. Mariánské; Metro: Staroměstská (A)*

Fred and Ginger (Tančící dům) (108/B6)

★ California star architect Frank O. Gehry and his colleague Vlado Milunič created the building in 1996 with two intertwining towers of concrete and glass. It was commissioned by a Dutch insurance company and is known colloquially in Prague as 'Fred Astaire and Ginger Rogers' due to its resemblance to a couple dancing. The American *Time* Magazine gave it the Best Design Award for 1996. It contains a luxury restaurant. *Rašínovo nábřeží 80, Metro: Karlovo náměstí (B)*

'House at the Stone Bell' (U kamenného zvonu) (108/C2)

Originally a Romanesque building from the 13th century, it was converted in 1325 to a city residence – presumably for Queen Eliška of the Přemyslid dynasty. Until 30 years ago the building still had a neo-Baroque façade, it then underwent a thorough restoration that uncovered a wealth of Gothic detail, testifying to the building's original splendour. This façade is without equal in central Europe. Ancient music and modern art exist in harmony in the beautiful halls and chapels. On the left wall of the entrance hall is a statue of a so-called 'Venus With a Mocking Smile' (in the words of Johannes Urzidil), with a globe between her thighs, and her index finger pointing to her lap. The rather frivolous caption originally read: 'It is around this point that the Earth revolves.' *During exhibitions daily (except Mon); 10 am–6 pm; Staroměstské náměstí 13; Metro: Staroměstská (A).*

Loreta Shrine (101/D5)

★ After the defeat of the Protestant army in the battle of White Mountain (1620), the Habsburgs wanted the population to again embrace the Catholic Church. To encourage conversion, beautiful churches and monuments were erected. One of the most outstanding of these was the Loreto Shrine, the jewel of the Bohemian Counter Reformation. At the centre of this sanctuary is the Loreto Chapel, a replica of the Casa Santa de Loreto in Italy.

The Prague 'Casa Santa' (Holy House) was commissioned by Princess Lobkovicz and built between 1626 and 1631 by Giovanni Battista Orsi. Inside is a silver altar and a Madonna carved from cedar wood. The 'Casa Santa' is surrounded by a cloister. In the Chapel of the Virgin Mary, to the right of the entrance, is the famous statue of the bearded St Wilgefortis. According to legend this Portuguese princess did not wish to surrender her virginity and prayed to heaven to be given a beard, upon which her father had her crucified. The western front tract with the tower was built by the Dientzenhofers, both father and son. Every hour the carillon plays an old Bohemian canticle to the Virgin Mary, as it has done for the past 300 years. The vault houses some extraordinary treasures. There are 300 priceless exhibits in all, the most spectacular of which is the Diamond Monstrance (1698), with 6222 diamonds, weighing 12kg. It was a gift from Countess Ludmila Kolowrat.

Daily except Mon, 9–12 am and 1–5 pm; Loretánské náměstí 7; Metro: Hradčanská (A)

Municipal House
(Obecní dům) (109/E2)

Until the beginning of the 20th century, the Royal Court, stood on this site. The front of the magnificent Art Nouveau Municipal House (1906-1911) is adorned with a mosaic entitled *Homage to Prague*. This 'House of Representation', renovated between 1995 and 1997, contains six concert and dance halls, two restaurants and a café. The lovely Smetana Hall provides the stage for the opening concert of the 'Prague Spring Festival'. It is a place of historic significance: it was here that Czechoslovak independence was declared on 28th October 1918. *A group tour with a guide can be booked at the information kiosk on the first floor, or*

Cubism in Prague

In 1909-1925, the works of the Francophile Czechs are not orientated to Expressionism, but Cubism. Works, among others, from Kubišta and Gutfreund are to be found in the National Gallery. The Cubist buildings are worth seeing: Celetná 34 (**109/D2**), the double house at Tychonova 268 (**101/E4**), the Villa on the corner of the Libušina Road (**105/F3**) and three houses at Rašínovo nábřeží 6, 8, 10 (**105/F3**). A beautifully formed Cubist streetlight stands near to the Wenceslas Square next to the Church of St Mary of the Snows (**109/D3**). Cubist furniture is found nowhere else in the world except in the Prague Museum of Arts and Crafts.

Tel: 22 00 21 01, Náměstí Republiky 5, Metro: Náměstí Republiky (B)

New World (Nový svět) (101/D5)
Behind the Hradschin you can discover, like Columbus, the New World. You walk from Loreto Square past the Černín Palace and the Loreto Shrine to the Capuchin Church with its black indentations in the façade, made by Friedrich II's cannonballs. The Černín Palace, today the Foreign Ministry, lies to the left, the Loreto Shrine to the right. You come into a magical spot from the 16th century where tourists are seldom found. In the year 1600 Johannes Kepler ran down over these cobblestone when he wished to visit his friend, the Danish astronomer Tycho Brahe, at 1 Nový svět (memorial plaque). Both carried out their observation of the planets at Emperor Rudolf II's Hradschin Court. The little lane, Nový svět, is a center for artists today. *Metro: Malostranská (A); Tram No. 22; Pohořelec stop.*

Old Town Bridge Tower (Staroměstská mostecká věž) (108/B2)
⚜ Built next to the Charles Bridge in 1391 to plans by Peter Parlers, this is one of the most impressive gothic bridge towers in Europe. Above the portal you can still make out the coats of arms of ten countries once belonging to the Bohemian kingdom, together with a veil and kingfisher, the symbol of King Wenceslas IV. The statues of the bridge's patron, St Vitus, were also made in Parler's workshop: St Vitus, protector of the bridge, is flanked by Charles IV on the right and Wenceslas IV on the

left, above them stand St Sigismund and St Vojtěch (Adalbert). The decorations on the waterfront were destroyed by the Swedes with heavy artillery back in 1648.
Daily 9 am–7 pm; Karlův most, The Charles Bridge; Metro: Staroměstská (A)

Old Town Hall (Staroměstská radnice) (108/C2)
In 1338, King John of Luxembourg gave the Old Town permission to build its own town hall. The costs were to be met by the introduction of a new wine tax. The inhabitants must have liked their drink, for within the same year they raised enough funds to acquire an early Gothic corner house. Some years later they erected the Town Hall Tower (69m/228ft) as a symbol of the secular power of the city.

The Astronomical Clock on the Old Town Hall, showing the hourly procession of the apostles

On the south side is the ★ Astronomical Clock (1410), with the famous Procession of the Apostles, indication of the phases of the moon, and the positions of the planets. On every full hour the old clockwork begins a scenario from 10 am to 10 pm, in which Death appears holding an hourglass and sounding the death knell. The Twelve Apostles also appear, in alternation, in the two little windows to the right and left: Paul, Peter, Thomas, Matthew, Judas, John, Simon, Andrew, Bartholomew, Philip, Barnabas, and Jacob. A Turk shakes his head because he does not wish to abandon the wars of conquest. The Miser proudly shakes his sack of money, and Vanity admires itself in a mirror. In 1621, 27 Protestant leaders of an uprising against the Catholic Habsburgs were decapitated on the east side of the building. The Kingdom of Bohemia lost its independence for the next 300 years. Many citizens of Prague lose their personal freedom in this house today: numerous weddings take place in the Town Hall.
Daily 9 am–5.30 pm, PIS information at the Town Hall, Staroměstské náměstí; Metro: Staroměstská (A)

Powder Tower (Prašná brána) (109/E2)

The Powder Tower (1475), actually the Powder Portal, marks the beginning of the Coronation Procession in the Old Town. The architect and stonemason Matouš Rejsek furnished this building with delightful and rich decoration. At the end of the 17th century, the tower served as a store for gunpowder and it has since been known as the Powder

The Powder Tower in the Old Town

Tower. The view from above over the roofs of the Old Town is very rewarding. Before the Second World War the 'Ladies of the Powder Tower' were a familiar sight in this area: it was from here that they lured their customers to their shabby little rooms in the Old Town.
April–August, 9 am–7 pm; Náměstí Republiky; Metro: Náměstí Republiky (B)

Rudolfinum (108/B1)

The Rudolfinum (1876-1884) which was built by Josef Zítek und Josef Schulz, the architects of the National Theatre, is the

SIGHTSEEING

loveliest neo-Renaissance memorial in Prague. Named in honour of Crown Prince Rudolf, it was opened with a concert conducted by Antonín Dvořák. A magnificent staircase leads to the monumental columned hall, which in turn leads to the architecturally superb Dvořák Hall which holds an audience of 1200 and has excellent acoustics. The second part of the building houses an interesting art gallery which one enters through a large neo-Renaissance foyer. The square on which the Rudolfinum stands is named after the philosophy student who set fire to himself in Wenceslas Square in 1969 in protest of the Soviet invasion. *Daily except Mon, 10 am–6 pm, Metro: Staroměstská (A)*

BRIDGES

Čech bridge (Čechův most) (102/B4)
The graceful Art Nouveau Cechův Bridge (1906-1908) forms a logical finish to the beautiful Pařížská Avenue. Of particular interest are the decorative figures holding the lamps, as well as the Victory figures. *Metro: Staroměstská (A)*

Charles Bridge (Karlův most) **(108/A–B2)**
★ ☼ ⚅ In 1357, Emperor Charles IV had a new Gothic bridge built almost on the same site as the former Romanesque Judith Bridge (1167-1342). It is the work of Peter Parler and rests on 16 columns, it is 520m (1720ft) long and 10m (33ft) wide. This predominantly Baroque avenue of statues was constructed in the years between 1683 and 1714. Artistically, the

most valuable among these statues is that of St Luitgard by Matthias Bernhard Braun: It shows Christ leaning down from the cross to the saints gathered below (12th statue on the left from the Old Town bridge tower). The most popular, frightening, and legend-laden is the horrifying figure of the cruel Turk by F. M. Brokoff: the Turk guards the imprisoned Christians (14th figure on the left). The best known is the bronze statue of St John of Nepomuk who became the patron saint of bridges throughout Catholic Europe (8th statue on the right). Touching the relief below the statue is said to bring luck – it must really be so, for French President Jacques Chirac touched it in 1997 and two months later his party lost the election. Between the sixth and seventh columns a cross marks the spot where the saint was thrown into the river 600 years ago. Standing near the figure of St Cajetán (12th statue on the right) one has a lovely view over Kampa Island with Prague's 'Little Venice.' This bridge often played a part in the country's history. Frederick V fled across it in 1620 after his defeat at White Mountain, and the heads of twelve Protestant nobles kept a grisly watch over the bridge as they hung from the Old Town bridge tower for ten years following their execution in the Old Town Ring. The people of Prague fought against the Swedes on the Charles Bridge in 1648. In 1848, the year of revolution, barricades were set up here by the Prague revolutionaries, 43 of whom lost their lives in the city. The bridge today has become a true 'Prague Montmartre' lined with hawkers, portrait artists and musicians. The two bridge towers on the Little Quarter bank are connected by a portal. In the sandstone wall to the left, at a height of around three metres, one can see deep grooves – it was here that the Swedes sharpened their halberds. The lower tower was part of the fortifications of the Judith Bridge, the higher was built in 1464. *Viewing tower: Daily from April to October 10 am–6 pm; Nov to March 10 am–5 pm; Karlův most, Metro: Staroměstská (A)*

CEMETERIES

New Jewish Cemetery (Nový židovský hřbitov) (O)

Franz Kafka and his parents, Hermann and Julia Kafka, are buried in this cemetery. *Thurs and Sun 9.15 am–3.30 pm; Fri 9–12.30 am; Žižkov, Nad vodovodem 1, Metro: Želivského (A)*

Old Jewish Cemetery (Starý židovský hřbitov) (108/C1)

★ This cemetery is one of the most important sights in Prague and has an important place among Jewish burial grounds world-wide. The oldest grave dates back to 1439, the most recent is dated 1787. The hilly location was due to a shortage of space (the cemetery is only 200m/660ft long), which led over the centuries to new graves being piled on top of old ones. In parts there are as many as nine graves on top of each other, containing the remains of at least 200,000 people. The 12,000 tombstones are a characteristic mixture of Gothic, Renaissance

and Baroque styles. Some of them feature elaborate reliefs in which the name of the deceased is often represented symbolically. Thus the tomb of Rabbi Löw – famous scholar and legendary creator of the Golem – is marked with a lion, and next to it is a pine cone, a symbol of immortality. Hands raised in blessing signify that the deceased was a member of a rabbinical family; jugs are the symbols of the Levites. Visitors to the cemetery place small stones rather than flowers on the graves, probably a custom from the desert, as a sign of their honour and respect. According to tradition one should, however, bring the small stones with one. It is recommended to take a tourist guide for a tour (Tel: 231 03 02). *Daily except Sat, 9.30 am–6 pm; U starého hřbitova 3a, Metro: Staroměstská (A)*

Vyšehrad (106/B4)

↙ From the rocky hill of Vyšehrad, Princess Libuše, the mythical founder of the city and progenitrix of the Přemyslid dynasty, predicted a glorious future for the city of Praha. This is also purported to be the site where the first Bohemian princes settled during the 10th century – archaeological excavations are continuous in the area. A Gothic fortress was built here in the 14th century and a Gothic church is mentioned in records. The castle was destroyed during the Hussite Wars. The castle ruins, the church of St Peter and St Paul and the Romanesque rotunda of St Martin can be seen to this day. After the ease with which the Swedes were able to invade the city at the end of the

Thirty Years War, a ⚔️ citadel with Baroque fortifications was built to replace the castle. During the Romanesque era, the legendary Vyšehrad regained notoriety as a symbol of Czech independence with the establishment of a national Slavín cemetery. On this Prague 'Père Lachaise' rests the writers Jan Neruda, Karel Čapek and Božena Němcová, the painter Mikoláš Aleš, the composers Bedřich Smetana and Antonín Dvořák, the violinist Jan Kubelík and his son, the conductor Rafael Kubelík who died in 1996.
Daily 9.30 am–5 pm; Soběslavova, Metro: Vyšehrad (C)

CHURCHES

Bethlehem Chapel
(Betlémská kaple)   (108/C3)
❖ This imposing, stark chapel, which could hold a congregation of 3000, was built between 1391 and 1394 for sermons delivered in the Czech language, rather than the traditional Latin. Its most interesting feature was originally not the altar but the pulpit from where the sermons were preached. At the end of the 14th century, when Bohemia was suffering a series of economic crises, the chapel became a popular forum for debate, which was undoubtedly about secular and spiritual power. It was in this chapel, between 1402 and 1412, that the reformist Jan Hus preached vociferously for the reformation of both the Church and social hierarchy. In 1415, he was condemned as a heretic and burnt at the stake in Constance – an execution that sparked the Hussite Wars. Demolished in the

18th century, the chapel was painstakingly rebuilt in 1953 with the help of the original plans. The walls are decorated with paintings based on miniatures from the *Jena Codex*.
Daily 9 am–6 pm; Betlémské náměstí, Metro: Národní třída (B)

Cathedral of St Cyril & Metodeje
(Kostel sv. Cyrila a
Metodĕje)   (108/C6)
❖ This church was originally built for the Roman Catholics by Kilian Ignaz Dientzenhofer between 1730 and 1736. Today it belongs to the Orthodox Church. During the Second World War it bore witness to one of Prague's most tragic chapters under Nazi dictatorship. Following the assassination in May 1942 of Richard Heydrich, second in command of the SS in the Third Reich after Himmler and Reichsprotektor of the Nazi state of Bohemia und Moravia, the seven Czech agents who orchestrated the killing took refuge in the church crypt. Heydrich's tyranny and his dark threats ('There is no room in Bohemia and Moravia for both Czechs and Germans ...') goaded the then London-based Czech government into sending paratroopers to Prague to carry out the assassination. Although the operation itself was successful, the reprisals were cruel. The Czech agents' hiding place was betrayed and 350 SS troops laid siege to the church for six hours. In the pitched battle 14 SS men were killed and 21 injured; three of the assassins were killed in the fighting and the other four shot themselves in the crypt. Immediately following Heydrich's assassination, 2300 Czechs were

executed out of hand. The crypt was recently declared a national monument to the victims of the 'Heydrichiade' and a memorial to reconciliation. *Tues to Sat 10 am– 4 pm, Resslova 9; Metro: Karlovo náměstí (B)*

Church of Panny Maria Victoria (Kostel P. Marie Vítězné) (101/E6)

The first Baroque church in Prague (1613) is known around the world, particularly in Italy, Spain, throughout Latin America and in the Philippines, for its effigy of the infant Jesus. On the marble altar on the right inner wall stands this famous wax statue, which originates from Spain. It was presented to the church as a gift from Polyxena of Lobkovicz in 1628. Many miraculous deeds have been attributed to the statue. The infant effigy has over 60 robes from all over the world, a velvet suit with golden embroidery was a gift from (and sewn by) the Empress Maria Theresia herself. The statue may only be dressed by nuns of the resident order – to witness this ceremony is a real experience. The church was given the name 'Victoria' following the victory of the Catholics over the Protestants at the battle of White Mountain (1620). After a concert in Prague, Plácido Domingo took along a copy of the Child Jesus as a souvenir. *Karmelitská ulice, Metro: Malostranská (A)*

Knight's Church (Kostel Křižovníků) (108/B3)

Also known as the Church of St Francis, it was built between 1578 and 1602 for the Knights of the Order of the Cross. An unimpressive entrance leads to a valu-

able collection of the Order's treasures, also the underground St Francis Chapel, and a well-preserved arch of the Judith Bridge (1167-1342), precursor of the Charles Bridge, on display for the first time in 1995 after centuries of being hidden. *Křižovnické náměstí 3, Metro: Staroměstská (A)*

St Mary of the Snows (Kostel Panny Marie Sněžné) (109/D3)

Founded by Charles IV as the Coronation Church in 1347, it was meant to surpass St Vitus Cathedral in size, with a length of more than 110m (360ft). The high, brightly lit and breathtaking Presbytery – at 35m (115ft) the tallest church building in Prague – was completed in 1397. The actual building was never finished due to the Hussite Revolution. Inside on the left is the highest main altar in Prague (1625), with the painting *The Annunciation* by Václav Vavřinec Reiner and a pewter baptismal font (1459) at the entrance. The church became a centre of the radical wing of the Hussites. In the year 1419 the priest Jan Želivský gathered a procession of Prague's poorest and marched from Wenceslas Square along the Štěpánská to the Nové Mesto town hall where the crowd threw the councillors out of the windows, marking the first Prague Defenestration. This spark lit the flames of the Hussite Revolution (1419-1434). *Jungmannova náměstí, Metro: Můstek (A und B)*

St Jacob's Church (Kostel sv. Jakuba) (109/D2)

This originally Romanesque church was destroyed by fire and

subsequently rebuilt in the Gothic style in 1366. Between 1689 and 1739 it was again transformed, this time in high Baroque style. Behind the sumptuous front decoration with carved reliefs of St Jacob, Francis and Anthony, the imposing interior is decorated with 21 carved high altars featuring paintings by Petr Jan Brandl. Above the main altar hangs the painting *The Matyrdom of St Jacob* by Václav V. Reiner. The colossal tomb of the High Chancellor of Bohemia, Vratislav von Mitrovice (†1712) is the most beautiful in Prague and was made according to plans by Fischer von Erlach. It is worth visiting the church during mass or a concert to fully appreciate the remarkable acoustics. The organ, the largest Baroque organ in Prague, has 4 manuals and 95 registers. *Malá Stupartská 8, Metro: Náměstí Republiky (B)*

St Niklas Church
(Chrám sv. Mikuláše) (101/E5)
★ The building of the Church of St Niklas (1703-1756) marked the apogee of Bohemian high Baroque. It became for the Jesuits the symbol of their triumph and jubilation over the country's return to Catholicism. The nave was built with marvellous boldness by Christoph Dientzenhofer, the massive cupola was the work of his son Kilian Ignaz, and the slender 75m (250ft) bell tower was built by the latter's son-in-law Anselm Lurago. The tower offers a wonderful view of the city. ☙ From here a variation of the Stasi secret police watched and listened in on the 'imperialistic' embassies during communist times. The monumental ceiling fresco above the nave by Jan Lukas Kracker depicts the glorification of St Niklas. It is one of the largest painted ceilings in Europe. The fresco in the cupola portraying the glorification of the Holy Trinity was painted by Franz Xaver Balko. The four enormous statues under the cupola, and the golden statue of Nicholas above the main altar, are the work of the Prague-born Rococo sculptor Ignác Platzer. The church is bursting with hidden treasures. In the first lateral chapel on the left hangs a painting of the Holy Cross by the prominent Baroque painter Karel Skréta. Above the side altar on the left, on which stands the Gothic statue of the Virgin Mary from Foyen in Belgium (brought here from the well-known site of pilgrimage by the Jesuits), is a sculpture by Jan Lukas Kracker. In this figure he has immortalized a certain curious Jesuit who would peer at him from behind a half-open door. *Malostranské náměstí, Metro: Malostranská (A)*

St Thomas' Church
(Kostel sv. Tomáše) (101/E5)
This beautiful church, with its delicate spire, is not far from the Malá Strana. King Václav II laid the foundation stone in 1285 for the church and its monastery. The building was completed by the Augustine hermits in early Gothic style in 1379. The monastery was very rich, since the monks had been operating a brewery here since 1358. For nearly 600 years they brewed excellent black beer, using ancient recipes. In 1637 the prior J. Svitavský commissioned Peter Paul Rubens to paint two

pictures – *The Torment of St Thomas'* and *St Augustine*. The originals are now to be seen in the National Gallery, while the church exhibits copies. The church was rebuilt in Baroque style by Kilian Ignaz Dientzenhofer between 1723 and 1731, the magnificent interiors were created by renowned Bohemian artists and the main altar is by Kristián Kovár. The ceiling frescos are by Václav V. Reiner, the two large statues on the main altar are the work of Jan A. Quitainer. Around the corner in Tomášská Lane is a Baroque house (no 4), also by Dientzenhofer, with one of the finest house signs in Prague – showing St Hubertus with a deer – by Ferdinand Maximilian Brokoff. *Letenská ulice, Metro: Malostranská (A)*

Týn Church
(Týnský chrám)   (109/D2)
✪ With its two 80m (265ft) towers – the smaller one on the left is known as Eve, the larger on the right, Adam – and the sumptuous ornamentation, the Týn Church is one of the most important monuments of the Bohemian Gothic period. Built between 1365 and 1511, it became the headquarters of the Prague Utraquists – moderate Hussites – who practised holy communion 'in both forms' (bread and wine) whence their choice of the chalice as a symbol. The giant, heavily gilded chalice, which held 400 litres (approx. 100 gallons) and which the Hussite king Jiří z Poděbrad had placed next to his statue in the high stone gable, was melted down in the 17th century and its gold was reworked into a statue of the Virgin Mary. The beautiful

tympanum over the north portal depicts scenes from Christ's Passion. In the interior – gloomy for decades, but well lit since 1997 – it is worth keeping an eye out for the *Gothic Madonna and Child* on the wall of the right aisle (c. 1400), the late Gothic stone baldaquin by Matouš Rejsek (1493), the painting of *The Assumption* by Karel Skréta (on the main altar) and, to the right in front of the main altar, the marble gravestone of the Dane Tycho Brahe, astronomer to Emperor Rudolf II, who lost his nose in a duel. The north and south apses feature Gothic benches with corbels in the form of the heads of King Václav IV and his wife. *Staroměstské náměstí, Metro: Staroměstská (A)*

Černín Palace
(Černínský palác)   (101/D5)
The wealthy imperial ambassador in Venice, Count Humprecht Jan Černín z Chudenic, decided to build a palace in Prague which he could boast of to all the nobility of Europe. He chose the reputed architect Francesco Caratti, who constructed the 150m (500ft) long building with its 30 stately half-columns between 1668 and 1688. There is one story that encapsulates the Count's desperate quest for prestige: In September of 1673, the Emperor Leopold I was expected for the ceremony of laying the foundation stone of St Nicholas Church. Černín urged his architect to speed up the building process so that he could show the Emperor the greatest building ever constructed north of the

24

Alps. Instead of being impressed, the Emperor was insulted, as the Count had thus outshone his own royal castle in Vienna. The Count invested 100,000 florins in the first phase of building alone – no one knows what the final bill amounted to. In 1742 the French army plundered the palace and in 1757 the Prussians severely damaged it during a heavy bombardment. In the early years of the Czechoslovak Republic (1928-34) the palace was reconstructed, and it became the seat of the Foreign Ministry. The garden which was newly opened in 1997 was designed by Anselm Lurago – who also built a garden pavilion – in the 18th century. It has since not been spared the irony of the locals. Once a tourist was heard to ask, 'How many people actually work in this building?', to which a local replied, 'About half of them.' *Loretánské náměstí 5, Metro: Hradčanská (A), Tram 22*

Kinský Palace
(Palác Kinských) (109/D2)
This beautiful palace in the Staroměstské náměstí was built between 1755 and 1765 in the late Baroque style. It features unusual (for Prague) Rococo elements by Anselm Lurago, inspired by the designs of Kilian Ignaz Dientzenhofer, the architect of the church of St Nicholas opposite. From 1786 to 1945 the palace belonged to the Counts Kinský. A balcony, supported by two colonnaded doorways, runs across almost the entire front of the building. Countess Berta Kinský, the first woman to win the Nobel Peace Prize (1905), was born here. The palace was

also home to the Kafka family, during its time as the Austro-Hungarian Imperial *Deutsche Altstädter Gymnasium*, when the young Franz attended school. The rooms on the ground floor on the south-west side of the building housed the shop of one 'Hermann Kafka, Wholesale Haberdashers'. During the Czechoslovak Republic the salesman bohemianized his name to Heřman. Today the palace contains the graphic art collection of the National Gallery which comprises around 150,000 items. It frequently hosts exhibitions. *Staroměstské náměstí 12, Metro: Staroměstská (A)*

Liechtenstein Palace -
Lichtenštejnský palác (101/F6)
Queen Elizabeth and the Duke of Edinburgh stayed here during their official visit in March 1996. Royal English connections go back to the time of Charles IV (1346–1378) whose daughter, Princess Anna, married the English King Richard II and became known as 'Good Queen Ann'. The palace now houses a concert hall, a gallery and a café. *Kampa No. 506, Metro: Malostranská (A)*

Lobkovicz Palace
(Lobkovický palác) (101/E5)
Looking southwards from the castle parapet, you can make out the upper section of the Lobkovicz Palace, built at the beginning of the 18th century in early Baroque style by Giovanni Batista Alliprandi. In 1753, it came into the possession of the Lobkovicz family, who laid out a large English garden behind it. When it later housed the West German embassy, the palace gar-

dens became a refuge for thousands of East German citizens, who abandoned their Trabants and Wartburgs in the neighbouring streets. A Czech artist painted one of these 'Trabis' in gold, fitted it with long legs and placed it in the Lobkovicz Gardens. In memory of these events the German foreign minister unveiled a plaque here in October 1994. *Vlašská 19, Metro: Malostranská (A)*

Morzin Palace
(Morzinský palác) (101/E5)
The steep lane of Nerudova is not only notable for its house signs – such as *The Golden Cups, The Ass at the Manger, The Red Lion* and *The Two Suns* – but also for the Morzin Palace. Its architectural design by Giovanni Santini and the sculpture by Ferdinand Maximilian Brokoff make this one of the finest palaces in Prague. The balcony is supported by two moors – the heraldic motif of the Morzin family. Over the doorway are two busts representing Night and Day. The balustrade is decorated with allegorical figures of the four continents. Australia had not yet been discovered when the palace was built in 1713-14. *Nerudova ulice 5, Metro: Malostranská (A)*

Smiricky Palace
(Palác Smiřických) (101/E5)
At the end of the 16th and the beginning of the 17th centuries, Europe was like a time bomb waiting to explode. In almost every country were violent clashes between Catholics and Protestants. The Continent was divided into two powerful ideological blocks, the Catholic League and the Protestant Un-

ion. The Kingdom of Bohemia, in which 90% of the population were Protestant, was a prime example of a central European corporative state, ruled by a Protestant aristocracy. However, their rights were restricted by the two Catholic governors in the Bohemian Chancellery, representatives of the Catholic emperor in Vienna. On 22nd May 1618, Protestant leaders met at the Smiřický palace and decided to dispose of the imperial governors – the Counts Martinic and Slavata – in Prague Castle. The day after the meeting Protestants marched to the Bohemian Chancellery and threw the governors out of the 16m (54ft) high windows (the 'Second Prague Defenestration'). This uprising of the Bohemian Protestants sparked off the Thirty Years' War. *Malostranské náměstí 18, Metro: Malostranská (A)*

PARKS AND GARDENS

Castle Gardens
(Hradní zahrady) (101/E5)
The gardens can be reached by way of the Bull Staircase, designed by Josip Plečnik, who also remodelled the rampart gardens. The huge granite bowl, weighing 40 tons, in the Paradise Garden is well worth seeing, as is the ◥▨ viewing terrace of the South Garden. Below the so-called Ludwig Wing, two obelisks mark the spot where Counts Slavata and Martinic, the two Habsburg governors who were victims of the 'Second Defenestration' in 1618, were fortunate enough to land safely on the dung heap below. *Metro: Hradčanská (A)*

Castle Terrace Gardens (Hradní terasovité zahrady) (101/E5)

★ The jewel in the crown of Prague's gardens are terrace-like areas with delightful gloriettes, wells and balconies which rise up on the castle hill. The Ledebour Garden and the large and small Palffy Gardens were re-opened in 1995 with the assistance of a special foundation set up under the patronage of Britain's Prince Charles and President Václav Havel. The enchanting Sala Terrena designed by F. M. Kaňka in the early 18th century, today provides a wonderful venue for chamber music concerts.

Valdštejnská 3, daily 10 am–10 pm; Metro: Malostranská (A)

Franciscan Garden (Františkánská zahrada) (109/D4)

The peaceful monastery gardens of St Mary of the Snows were laid out at the same time as the New Town (1348). Since the beginning of the 17th century the whole estate has belonged to the Franciscan friars. The gardens have recently been decorated with lamps and sculptures: the lovely Davídek (little David) portrays the natural power of water, three nymphs float on the surface, and a bust of the legendary Aesop stands on the ground nearby. The high chancel of the church is particularly impressive when viewed from the gardens.

Metro: Můstek (A und B)

Kampa (101/E6)

★ ☙ The romantic island of Kampa is separated from Malá Strana by a small strip of water, known as Čertovka (the devil's stream). On the northern side of the Charles Bridge, the Čertovka flows past a small cluster of houses – this is the 'Little Venice' of Prague. This peaceful island – also known as the Island of love – is the perfect place for a quiet stroll through the gardens and offers enticing views over the Vltava, the Charles Bridge and the National Theatre. If you are lucky, you might catch a glimpse of a flock of swans floating on the other side of the river.

Metro: Malostranská (A)

Royal Gardens (Královská zahrada) (101/E4)

◉ An Italian gardener named Francesco designed these beautiful Renaissance gardens in 1535 for Emperor Ferdinand I. In addition to the magnificent flowers and some exotic plants, the first tulips in Europe – brought to Prague by Busbek, the Emperor's ambassador in Constantinople – were cultivated here by the Emperor's personal physician and botanist, P. O. Mathioli. Originally built in 1569 for ball games, the Míčovna, richly decorated with fine sgraffito, was later used for parties, masked balls and plays. It has recently been turned into an art gallery. The delightful *Allegory of the Night* in front of the Míčovna is from the workshop of Matthias Braun. Rudolf II had animal cages erected in the Lion court. On the way to the Belvedere, there is a Baroque niche with a fountain and statue of Hercules (1670). In the 19th century, the garden was transformed into an English style landscape and now, after many years, it is once again open to the public.

Daily 10 am–5.45 pm; Hradschin; Metro: Hradčanská (A)

Vrtba Gardens
(Vrtbovská zahrada)   (101/E5)

This charming terrace garden (1725) is again open to the public after extensive renovation. To enter you will pass through a doorway and under an archway. You then walk uphill through a lovely Baroque garden (designed by F. M. Kaňka) scattered with jolly cherubs, vases and antique statues by Matthias Braun. Right at the top there is an observation terrace which offers an unusual ◁▷ view of the Little Quarter and Prague Castle. *Karmelitská 25, Metro: Malostranská (A)*

Waldstein Palace
(Valdštejnský palác)   (101/E5)

The largest and most splendid palace in Prague was built between 1624 and 1630 by the generalissimo of the imperial army, Albrecht Wenzel von Waldstein (the Wallenstein of Schiller's famous trilogy). His palace was intended as a counterpoint to Prague Castle. Wallenstein's forces – he put 100,000 men, the upkeep of which he could finance, at the disposal of the emperor – was so great that he aspired to the throne of Bohemia, so the emperor had him killed in the town of Cheb. The extensive gardens are laid out in the Sala Terrena style, unique in central Europe at the time. A vast loggia opens out to the gardens, and the paths are decorated with bronze statues by Adrian de Vries. These are actually copies; the originals were taken by the Swedes at the end of the Thirty Years' War (1648). There is a good view of the castle from the park. *Gardens, May–Sept. daily 9 am–7 pm; three entrances: Letenská, Valdštejnský Palace, next to the Metro station: Malostranská (A)*

SQUARES

Knights' Square
(Křižovnické náměstí)   (108/B2)

The Church of St Francis Seraphicus (on the left of the Charles Bridge), the Church of St Salvator and the Staré Mesto bridge towers enclose a small but picturesque square. A memorial to Charles IV, the founding charter in hand, was erected here to mark the 500th anniversary of the foundation of the Charles University. Designed by the Burgundian architect Mathey, the green-domed Knights' Church (see page 23) was built between 1679 and 1689. Christoph Willibald Gluck and Antonín Dvořák worked here as organists. Opposite the Charles Bridge stands the Renaissance church of St Salvator by Francesco Caratti and Carlo Lurago, with its Baroque portal (1572-1602) and twin towers, which were added later, designed by František Maximilian Kaňka. Peter Parler's Gothic bridge tower, often called the finest in Europe, completes the square. There is always something going on here: a wind quartet playing Baroque music, or a group of young people playing rhythmic jazz. *Metro: Staroměstská (A)*

Old Town Square
(Staroměstské náměstí)   (108/C2)

◉ This square has been an important commercial and political market place since the 12th century, when foreign merchants first convened from all quarters

The Jan Hus Memorial on the Old Town Square is a reminder of this important Reformer of the Middle Ages

of the globe at this 'crossroads to Bohemia' from the West and South. Behind the Týn church – on the masterly renovated Ungelt (literally, 'no money') – they paid duty on their goods since the 11th century and offered them for sale. The little square is dominated by the Granovský Palace with its Renaissance loggias. After 20 years of constant renovation work it was again opened in 1996. Prague is often referred to as the city of tragedy, since its cobblestones have been steeped in blood – the most notorious of several bloody events took place on 21st June 1621 when, after a failed uprising against the Habsburgs, 27 Bohemian and German noblemen and citizens were executed in front of the Town Hall. On the pavement, the spot where they fell is marked with 27 crosses. This event sealed Habsburg control over Bohemia for another 300 years. The St Niklas Church (1735) was built according to plans by K. I. Dientzenhofer. Jousting also took place in the square and to the delight of the spectating citizens, King Jan Lucemburský was once unseated here. A likeness of the great reformer Jan Hus, flanked by the oppressed and the defiant, looks from his immense memorial towards the Týn church where the first Reformation struggles began. The Gothic palace, 'House at The Stone Bell' with its beautiful façade, was home to the Přemyslid Eliška, heiress to Bohemia and mother of Charles IV. The magnificent coronation processions of the Bohemian kings would cross this square and march up to St Vitus Cathedral for the conferring of the royal title. The square has been impressively renovated; tourists stream to the town hall to admire the Astronomical Clock's hourly Parade of the Apostles (from 8 am to 8 pm).

In fine weather, visitors can immerse themselves in the wonderful ambience of these historical buildings as they sit under the colourful café umbrellas. During his stay in Prague from 1910–1911, Albert Einstein presented his theory of relativity at number 18, which was then a literary salon run by Berta Fanta and frequented by Kafka and others; it now houses the Café Amadeus.
Metro: Staroměstská (A)

Wenceslas Square
(Václavské náměst) (109/D3–E4)

★ ☺ Originally, this square which measures 750m x 60m (2250ft x 200ft), was a horse market. It represented a classic example of urban planning under Charles IV. Today it is more like an elegant boulevard than a square, and in recent history it has become something of a political seismograph for the nation. Lined with hotels, cinemas, restaurants, cafés and businesses, the square forms together with adjacent streets what is known as the Golden Cross, with the Na příkopě (jokingly called Prague's Wall Street due to its profusion of banks), Na Můstku, 28. října and Národní třída. At the top end of the square is the vast National Museum, in front of which stands the statue of Prince Václav, after whom the square is named, escorted by the equestrian statues of the national saints Ludmilla, Procopius, Agnes and Adalbert of Prague (by Vojtěch). It was near this monument in 1969 that Jan Palach committed suicide by setting himself alight, in protest at the Soviet occupation. The protests against the Communist regime were also concentrated around this square and it is here that the democratic revolution began.
Metro: Můstek (A and B), Muzeum (A and C)

Wenceslas Square: A stately boulevard with a great symbolic political power

PRAGUE CASTLE/HRADSCHIN

☞ Map of castle – inside back flap

★ ⇕ ☺ (101/E4–5) For more than a thousand years Prague Castle has been at the centre of the country's political life. The Guinness Book of Records lists it as the biggest castle in the world. It covers 7.2 hectares (17.8 acres), measuring 570m x 128m (1880ft x 425ft). Also for over a thousand years, this has been the secular and spiritual heart of Bohemia. Founded in about 880 AD, the Castle was built in the Romanesque style by the Přemyslids, and transformed by successive dynasties – Gothic by the Luxembourg princes, Late Gothic by the Jegiellons, and Renaissance and Baroque by the Habsburgs. The last rebuilding work (1753-1775) gave the castle its current Classical form. After the founding of the Czechoslovak Republic in 1918 the castle once again became a symbol of statehood and the presidential headquarters. In 1989, poet and former state enemy number one Václav Havel and took up residence here as president. *Guided tours of the castle; information is available in the second courtyard Chapel of the Holy Cross. Tel: 33 37 33 68; Metro: Hradčanská (A)*

The Castle

The main entrance is on the Hradčanské náměstí, through gates decorated with two *Battling Titans* by the sculptor Ignác Platzer, into the main courtyard where the changing of the guard (12 am) is worth seeing. Above the equally monumental Baroque Matthias Gate (1614) to the right, the presidential flag, bearing the state coat of arms and Hussite slogan *Pravda vitezí* ('Truth Prevails'), flies when the president is in residence. In the middle of the second courtyard is a Baroque fountain, and to the right the Chapel of the Holy Cross and castle information point. Immediately at the front left is the entrance to the Castle gallery, which has recently been reopened, with the remains of the Emperor's excellent art gallery, a total of 70 works: Rubens, Titian, Veronese, Tintoretto, von Aachen, Braun, Kupecký, and Brandl. The remains of a late 9th century Church of Mary were discovered here. Behind the passage one comes into the third and most important courtyard, and thus to the west portal of St Vitus Cathedral. A 16m (53ft) monolith, a memorial to the vic-

tims of the First World War, stands impressively to the right. The lively statue of a horse and rider from 1373 depicts St George fighting the Dragon. On the north side of the castle behind the entrance to the second courtyard one crosses the deep stag moat, used for breeding game. A part of it forms the Lion Court (Lví dvůr), the animal cages that Rudolf had built to hold lions, tigers and bears. According to the prophesy of the astronomer Tycho Brahe the ailing emperor would expire shortly after the death of his favourite lion. Prophesy became reality – the ruler died two days after the beast. *Castle: April 1– Oct. 31, daily 5 am–midnight; buildings 9 am–5 pm; Nov. 1 to March 31, daily 6 am–11 pm; buildings 9 am– 4 pm; the gardens are closed in winter.*

St Vitus Cathedral

❂ The cathedral is the most important sacred building in Prague. It was used for coronations and as burial place of kings, and later as the treasure vault for the Bohemian coronation insignia. To build the perfect setting, Charles IV called in two brilliant architects, the Frenchman Matthew of Arras and, after the latter's death in 1352, Peter Parler. Construction began in 1344, and was interrupted by the beginning of the Hussite War in 1420. During this time, only the chancel and the foundations of the main tower were built. ◁ The tower rises to 99 m (325 ft) and houses the Sigismund Bell (1549) — at 17,000kg (37,500lbs) it is the biggest church bell in Bohemia. The tower was built in Gothic style and finished in Renaissance

The portal to St Vitus Cathedral, the coronation church of the Bohemian kings

and Baroque style. One of the true gems of Gothic architecture in Prague is the Triforium (1371–75), which runs completely around the chancel. Sun streams into the cathedral through the large glass rosette (*The Creation of the World*) with a diameter of 10.4m (35ft), and the artistically designed stained-glass windows – one of the loveliest is by Alfons Mucha in the third chapel left from the entrance. Also on the left is the altar with the *Crucified* (1899) by František Bílek. The cathedral is 124m (410ft) long, 60m (200ft) wide and 34m (112ft) high and was finally completed to Parler's original plans in 1929.

Wenceslas Chapel

Among the most noble rooms is the Wenceslas Chapel, the heart of the cathedral and the highpoint of Bohemian Gothic. Peter Parler built it between 1362 and 1364 exactly on the site of the original St Vitus Rotunda (925) in which its builder, the national patron St Wenceslas, was laid to rest. The wall – described from the bottom to the top – is decorated with 1345 polished Bohemian semi-precious gems, with frescos depicting the passion of Christ, and at the top with scenes from the Wenceslas legend in the Renaissance style. On a ledge above the altar stands the Gothic statue of St Wenceslas (1373).

Coronation Chamber

Above the Chapel lies the Coronation Chamber, which serves as the treasury of the Bohemian crown jewels. The chamber door is fitted with seven locks that can only be opened by the seven holders of the keys – including the president and the parliament speaker – acting in concert. The crown is encrusted with 91 gems and 20 pearls and weighs 2.5kg (5.5lbs). The coronation insignia are seldom exhibited.

Royal Crypt

The Royal Crypt contains the sarcophagi of Charles IV and his four wives, as well as Wenceslas IV, Ladislaus Posthumus and Jiří Poděbradys, as well as the tin sarcophagus of Rudolf II.

Imperial Mausoleum and Choir

In front of the high altar in the chancel is the white marble Renaissance sarcophagus (1564–1581), with three figures – Ferdinand I, his wife Anna and their son Maximilian II. The carved wooden relief panelling (1630) on either side of the altar shows the flight of Frederick V after his defeat at the Battle of White Mountain and the plundering of the cathedral by Calvinists in 1619. To the right of the altar stands the magnificent 3700kg (8150 lbs) solid silver tomb of St John of Nepomuk, built (1733-1736) from extravagant designs by Fischer von Erlach. The Zlatá Brána (Golden Gate) leads back to the third courtyard, where the Gothic bronze statue (1373) of St George stands. The front wall of the cathedral is decorated with a 14th century Gothic mosaic of the *Last Judgement* (1370-1371), which Czech experts restored in co-operation with the Getty Institute in Los Angeles.

Vladislav Hall

Be sure to see the beautiful Vladislav Hall in the former Royal Palace. The 62m (204ft) long, 16m (53ft) wide and 13m (43ft) high hall was built between 1493 and 1502 by Benedikt Ried. With its sweeping rib vaulting, it is the most grandiose hall of the late medieval period – its windows, however, are in early Renaissance style. This is where the Bohemian kings received homage from their vassals, and where coronation festivities complete with jousting events were held. Until 1993 this was also where the head of state was elected. Note the Gothic curve of the flat-stepped staircase that served as the entrance for participants in the jousting events. Below the hall is a 14th century Gothic hall named in honour of the Emperor Charles.

Bohemian Chancellery

In the Ludvíc Wing next to the Vladislav Hall are the rooms of the Bohemian Chancellery, where, in 1618, following a brief argument, the Protestant nobles threw the two imperial governors and their secretary Fabricius out of the castle windows. The victims received grace of a special kind: a dung heap saved the Counts Martinic, Slavata, and Fabricius, later knighted by the emperor (ironically) as 'Sir Highflight.' This 'Second Prague Defenestration' marked the beginning of the Bohemian uprising and led to the Thirty Years War.

Basilica of St George

The Basilica of St George is the oldest and best preserved Romanesque church in Bohemia. It was founded in 920 by Prince Vratislav I and ceremoniously dedicated in 925 as the burial chapel of St Ludmilla, the grandmother of St Wenceslas. Fifty years later a Benedictine convent was founded here; its abbess was Princess Mlada. The abbess had the right to place the crown upon a queen's head at her coronation. On the front wall of the main nave are the gravestones of the Přemyslid rulers Vratislav and Boleslav, and in the chapel is the tomb of St Ludmilla. To the right at the exit is the permanent exhibition 'Ancient Bohemian Art.'

The Black Tower

The Black Tower which stands at the end of Golden Lane dates from the first half of the 12th century. Charles IV had the rooftops of the Black and White Towers covered with gold foil, so that they would gleam over the city, possibly giving rise to the name 'The Golden City'.

The White Tower and the Mihulka Tower

A notorious state prison, the White Tower held such prisoners as the English magician E. Kelley and the imperial valet K. Rucky, who hanged himself with the same gold rope used to hang up the key to the imperial treasury (to which the disloyal servant had been granting himself liberal access). Today, it houses an extensive glass exhibition. A permanent display in the Mihulka Tower shows an alchemist's kitchen dating from the time of Rudolf II. It also features the golden vessel in which the king's brain was kept.

Golden Lane   (101/E4)

This picturesque blind alley is one of the most popular sights in Prague. It has also been called Alchemists' Alley since legend has it that the alchemists who lived in these little cottages used to produce the philosophers' stone, the elixir of life and, above all, gold for Emperor Rudolf II. In fact, it was the bowmen of the castle guards who resided here, followed later by goldsmiths. One of the houses (No. 22) served as a temporary refuge for Franz Kafka in 1917 while he was writing his short stories. A little further down (at No. 14) lived the clairvoyant Madame de Thèbe (whose real name was Matylda Prošová), who prophesied the Nazi defeat and was beaten to death by the Gestapo during an interrogation.

Daliborka Tower

At the end of the lane is a prison tower which bears the name of the rebel Dalibor. According to legend he learned to play the violin in prison to such perfection that many came from the city to listen to him. In 1498, however, the violin was silenced. Dalibor was beheaded. Bedřich Smetana used this story for the theme of his opera "Dalibor".

DISTRICTS

Josefov (Židovské město) (108/C1)

Over 1000 years ago, Jewish merchants settled in Prague – all other occupations except trade were forbidden them. A Jewish settlement was first established in the area around the Old Synagogue during the 13th century. The term 'ghetto' first came into use in the 16th century. The settlement became a town, with separate Jewish administration, and synagogues and schools were built. The community repeatedly fell prey to pogroms, most of which were provoked by the Catholic Church. The tolerant Emperor Rudolf II cultivated contact with the Jewish community; in 1592, he met with Rabbi Löw to discuss the secrets of astrology and mysticism. On several occasions, the exceedingly wealthy banker Mordechai Maisel lent the Emperor money for the war against the Turks and to enrich the imperial collections, through which the Emperor earned Prague the title of 'Art Capital of Europe'. At the end of the 19th century Josefov was renovated, old houses torn down and new ones built in their place. Jews were officially granted citizenship in 1848, after which time they could reside in other parts of the city. The old Jewish cemetery, the town hall,

and six synagogues survived the renovation. The cemetery is worth a visit and the synagogues now house some exceptional art collections, both religious and secular. These include some fabulous silver artefacts, a collection of tabernacle curtains and Torah scrolls from synagogues in Bohemia and Moravia pillaged by the Nazis, who intended to found a 'Museum of an Extinct Race'. During the Second World War, the Jewish community was virtually annihilated and today there are no more than approximately a thousand Jewish residents in Prague. The 'Jewish Museum' shows the extent to which the Jewish community contributed to culture and science.
Metro: Staroměstská (A)

Little Quarter (Malá strana)   (101/D–F 5–6)

The Little Quarter is situated on the left bank of the Vltava, in the triangle between the river and the two hills of Hradčany and Petřín, on the slopes below the Castle. The original small settlement of artisans and tradesmen was established in 1257 by Přemyslid King Otakar II as Prague's second town after Staré Město. Many battlements were constructed including the 'Hunger Wall', built under the Strahov Gardens in 1360 by Charles IV. Merchants, who became wealthy from their dealings with the royal court, and the German nobility who came here after their victory in the Battle of White Mountain gave the Little Quarter its architectural harmony. Next to the Church of St Nicholas with its green domes, the crowning achievement of Prague Baroque style, are the Baroque palaces of Valdštejn, Nostic, Buquoy, Thun, Furstenberg and Liechtenstein, all clustered at the foot of the Castle. There are many bourgeois Baroque houses, with emblems indicating the profession of their former occupants, as in the steep Nerudova Lane. Almost every lane in the Little Quarter is haunted – there is, for example, a headless Swedish soldier in Nerudova Lane who appears after midnight carrying his head under his arm. The people of the Little Quarter beheaded him in the Thirty Years War. The Little Quarter is famous for cosy old wine cellars in which good wine is served with excellent dishes. You can wander around this quarter for hours, view Kampa Island, or relax in the tranquil surroundings of the Strahovská or Seminářská Gardens. *Metro: Malostranská (A)*

New Town   (102–103/B–D 5–6) (Nové Město)   (106/B–C 2–3)

What is still known as the New Town was in fact founded by Charles IV nearly 650 years ago (1348). This semi-circular belt encloses the heart of the old city. The new town walls were completed in two years, thus tripling the size of the city. Three massive market squares were laid out: the Horse Market (Václavské náměstí – Wenceslas Square), the Cattle Market (Karlovo náměstí) and the Hay Market (Senovážné náměstí). Large streets were built and the area also has some delightful Gothic churches and monasteries. Building was encouraged through tax conces-

sions .The New Town bears witness to the genius of the imperial planners, since the medieval city's infrastructure is today able to withstand the demands of a modern city while remaining virtually unchanged.
Metro: Muzeum (A and C)

Old Town
(Staré Město) (108–109/B–D 1-4)
The Old Town is the heart of Prague and reveals much about the historical and architectural development of the city. About 1000 years ago, the Staroměstské náměstí was nothing more than a market square. Then in 1230 King Václav I granted tradesmen and craftsmen the right to build their homes around it and settlements were soon formed. At the time there were already over 40 Romanesque churches in Prague. Charles IV built some Gothic churches in the Old Town and in 1348 founded the first university in Central Europe here. Most of the original Romanesque and Gothic houses were redesigned under the influence of the magnificent Baroque style. Although the Old Town appears a little grey it has nevertheless kept its original charm and coherence of style. The historic buildings are interspersed here and there with modern ones such as the Cubist Dům U černé Matky boží (House of the Black Madonna), on Celetná 34, built in 1912 by Josef Gočár. At the turn of the century the Jewish Quarter,Josefov, was carelessly rehabilitated; fortunately, some of its beautiful monuments were spared. The fine Art Nouveau street of

Pařížská is now lined with airline offices and luxury shops, while many of the old houses along the Royal Route, Celetná and Husova have been converted into charming wine taverns. *Metro: Staroměstská (A)*

Guild Theatre
(Stavovské divadlo)   (109/D3)
The neo-classical building of the Guild Theatre was built in 1781-3 as a forum for entertaining the influential German community. Sixteen years later the Bohemian Guilds took it over and renamed it. Mozart chose this theatre for the premières of his operas *The Abduction from the Seraglio* and *The Marriage of Figaro*, to resounding success. He later wrote 'since the people of Prague understand opera so well, I will write one just for them'. On October 29th of that same year, the theatre staged the premiere of Mozart's new opera, *Don Giovanni*, under the baton of the composer personally. In January 1792, the theatre mourned Mozart's death and held a memorial performance starring his great admirer, the singer Josefina Dušková. Not surprisingly, director Milos Forman chose this theatre as a primary location for his award-winning film *Amadeus*. It was also the venue for the first Czech opera Dráteník by František Škroup, who was a director in the Guild Theatre from 1827 to 1857. The song *Where is my Home?* was later to become the national anthem and was heard here for the first time.

Between 1918 and 1938 both German and Czech performances were staged here, but in the Second World War, only German was permitted. After the war the building was renamed the Tyl Theatre after the composer of the national anthem. *Ovocný trh 6, Tel: 24 21 43 39, Metro: Mustek (A and B)*

Laterna Magika (108/B4)

Next to the National Theatre stands the glass-fronted Nová Scéna theatre (built 1977-1983), home to the reputed Laterna Magika company whose performances combine theatre, film, mime, dance and comedy. The Laterna Magika claims that its roots can be traced back to the late 16th century, during the reign of Rudolf II. It seems that Rabbi Löw — theologian, cabbalist and creator of the mythical figure of the Golem — once put on a show for Emperor Rudolf II in a darkened room using silhouettes of biblical patriarchs which were so lifelike that many in the audience took them for real. The first Laterna Magika show performed at the World Expo in Brussels back in 1958, turned out to be an overwhelming success. *Nová scéna, Národní třída 4, Tel: 24 91 41 29, Metro: Národní třída (B)*

National Theatre
(Národní divadlo) (108/B4)

The Neo-Renaissance National Theatre – known affectionately among the Czechs as 'The Golden Chapel on the Vltava', is probably the only theatre which was not built by the State, by the city, or by the ruling élite. It was built from funds donated by the entire Czech population, including the very poorest, who collected their pennies for several decades to build themselves a National Theatre base. It was designed by Josef Zítek, but tragedy struck when, shortly after construction was completed in 1881, a fire broke out and almost completely destroyed the building. In merely 47 days Prague's citizens joined forces once more to collect over one million florins, and two years later the theatre was officially opened. The greatest artists of the age contributed to the decor, both inside and outside. To date, the theatre has seen some 2500 performances of Smetana's opera *Libuše*. The National Theatre also stages ballets. *Národní třída 2; Tel: 24 91 26 73, Metro: Národní tříd (B)*

Prague State Opera
(Státní opera Praha) (109/F4)

The neo-classical theatre was built in 1886-7 by the Viennese architects Helmer and Fellner. It opened in 1888 as the New German Theatre with the inauguratiaon performance of Wagner's opera *Die Meistersinger*. At the front of the building, images of Dionysius and the muse Thalia stand above busts of Goethe, Schiller and Mozart. The interior is velvet and gold with beautiful plasterwork and decoration. Also staged here was the first complete performance of Wagner's *Ring*. The building was renamed the Smetana Theatre in 1945 and is now the State Opera. *Wilsonova 4, Tel: 26 53 53 and 24 22 98 98, Metro: Muzeum (A and C)*

Two hours in the museum

The extensive Prague art collections include Bohemian Gothic, Dürer's 'Feast of the Rosary', the diamond monstrance, nineteen Picassos and other Cubist works

Each year more than five million people flock to Prague's great museums and art galleries. The Sternberk Palace alone welcomes one million tourists annually and the same number visit the Jewish Museum in the Staré Město. But no trip to Prague is complete without seeing the modern art collection at the National Gallery, which reopened in 1995 after lengthy renovation. An extensive collection of 19th and 20th centuries. French art is displayed here alongside the work of Czech and other European artists of the 20th century. The National Museum and National Technical Museum also attract many visitors. Considering that the city has played, and continues to play, such a fundamental role in the history and development of music, there are several interesting museums dedicated to Mozart, Smetana and Dvořák which deserve to be seen. The Strahov Monastery Library, with its historic rooms, is a fascinating place, while a traditional exhibition venue is the Gothic towerhouse, U kamenného zvonmu ('The Stone Bell') on Staroměstské náměstí. More recently, art exhibitions have been held in the Míčovna in the Royal Gardens. The exhibition of old Bohemian art in St George's Monastery behind St Vitus Cathedral, and the Castle Gallery with works by Titian and Rubens are also worth a visit, especially for their Gothic masterpieces. If you prefer something more modern, a unique collection of Cubist furniture dating from the two first decades of the 20th century is housed in the Museum of Arts and Crafts. For a better understanding of Jewish religion and culture, take the guided tour of the Jewish Museum. English-speaking guides can be hired by the hour or by the day. Information and details on exhibitions are available from the PIS. All museums are open every day except Monday. *PIS: Na příkopě 20, Tel: 26 40 23, Metro: Můstek (A und B), and in the Old Town Hall, Tel: 24 48 22 02, Metro: Staroměstská (A)*

The National Museum in Wenceslas Square is a symbol of the Czech national renaissance

Agnes Convent (Anežský klášter)
Museum of 19th century
Czech art (102/B4)

The early Gothic convent of the order of the Poor Clares was founded in 1233 by the devout Czech princess St Agnes, daughter of the Přemyslid king Otakar I, who became its first abbess. After long and painstaking restoration work undertaken between 1963 and 1985, a museum housing some 500 exhibits was installed here. The Rococo, Classical, Romantic and Realist painting galleries are on the first floor of the former convent. The work of Josef Mánes – the central figure in 19th century Czech art – is surprisingly varied. The graceful painting *Josefina* is his most interesting work. The painters who decorated the National Theatre were dubbed as the 'National Theatre Generation'. Among them was Václav Brožík whose work *Hus at the Council in Constance* deserves special attention. Other artists represented here include Aleš, Marold, Pirner, Schwaiger, and Schikaneder, who prepared the way for Czech painting to move into the 20th century.

Daily (except Mon) from 10 am– 6 pm; U milosrdných 17, Metro: Náměstí Republiky (B)

Art Collection of Old Bohemia
(Staré české umění) (101/E5)

★ This gallery in St George's Monastery (973) features works from the 14th to 18th centuries, including some unique Gothic masterpieces. The basement holds the beautiful tympanum from St Mary of the Snows (1346), an equestrian portrait of St George (1373) and numerous Madonnas. A separate room displays the artistically magnificent but anonymous nine-part altarpiece showing scenes from the life of Christ. Another room is dedicated to panels (1357-67) by the artist Master Theodoric, whose talents were commissioned by the court of Charles IV. A further room is dominated by the votive painting of archbishop Jan Očko of Vlašim. On the ground floor are two tableaux with biblical themes (c. 380) by Master Trebon, Bohemia's most important Gothic artist. Mannerist works from the court of Rudolf II and the Baroque period are shown on the first floor. Works by Bartholomeus Spranger hang alongside portraits by Karel Škréta, and works by Petr Brandl, Jan Kupecký and Václav Vavřnec Reiner. Also represented are the master of High Baroque – the sculptor Matthias Braun and his contemporary, Ferdinand Maximilian Brokoff. *Daily (except Monday) 10 am–6 pm; Jiřský klášter, Metro: Hradčanská (A)*

Bertramka (Mozart Museum) (105/D3)

★ 🚶 Between 1787 and 1791, Mozart was a frequent guest at the Dušeks' summer residence. It was at Bertramka that he composed the overture (292 inspired bars) to the opera *Don Giovanni* the night before the opera's hugely successful inaugural performance in what was then Nostic (now Stavovské) Theatre. It was also here that, three months before his death, Mozart composed the aria *Io ti lascio, o cara, addio* for the diva Josefina Dušková. For the past 150 years, Bertramka has stood as a shrine to Wolfgang Amadeus Mozart, though the only physical vestiges of the great maestro exhibited in the house are 13 strands of Mozart's hair (the house as the composer knew it was ravaged by fire in 1871). Also on show are numerous letters, engravings, musical sketches, a grand piano, a two-manual cembalo, and a clavichord on which Mozart played arias from *Don Giovanni*. There is a reconstruction of Mozart's bedroom which features a beautiful painting on the ceiling. *Daily 9.30 am–16 pm; Mozartova 169, Metro: Anděl (B)*

Bilek Gallery (101/F4)

🚶 You shouldn't miss the chance to visit this unusual house and explore the extravagant and expressive works of the Art Nouveau and Symbolist sculptor František Bílek (1872-1941). The architecture of the house, which was built to the artist's design in 1912, is based on (and decorated after) the concept of a field of grain, and it was intended to be a 'cathedral of art' as much as it was a family residence. Among the artist's well-known sculptures are *Spiritual Encounter* and *Future Conquerors.* Though unfortunately he remains little known elsewhere, Bílek's work was admired by many of his Czech contemporaries, and by Franz Kafka in particular. *15 May–31 Oct. Daily except Monday; 10 am–5 pm; 1 Nov.–14 May, Sat. and Sun. 10 am–5 pm; Mickiewiczova 1, Metro: Hradčanská (A)*

Decorative Arts Museum (Uměleckoprůmyslové muzeum) (108/C1)

★ This fantastic glass, porcelain and ceramic collection consists of more than 16,000 exhibits from antiquity to the present day. Particularly worth seeing are the worked gold articles, a collection of clocks and timepieces from around 1600 and the collection of Czech cubist furniture dating from 1910 to 1923. *Daily except Mon. 10 am–6 pm; Ul. 17. listopadu 2, Metro: Staroměstská (A)*

Dvořák Museum (105/C3)

This Museum dedicated to the great composer Antonín Dvořák (1841-1904) was opened in 1932. It is housed in the Baroque summer villa *Amerika* built between 1712 and 1720 by the renowned architect Kilian Ignaz Dientzenhofer. Dvořák was the artistic director of the New York Conservatory from 1892 to 1895 and was in the United States when he wrote his famous ninth *New World Symphony. Daily except Monday. 10 am–5 pm; Ke Karlovu 20, Metro: I.P. Pavlova (C)*

Historical Exhibition of the National Museum (Historická expozice Národního muzea) (101/E5)

Across from the Castle, the Lobkovicz Palace houses a permanent exhibition on the development of Bohemia from prehistoric times to the present day. The exhibition is in a total of 18 halls. Amongst the oldest artefacts displayed are numerous Celtic finds. At one time, the Přemyslid kings had 60,000 miners producing silver for coinage. An interesting collection of Renaissance jewellery (and noteworthy replicas of the Bohemian crown jewels), selected clocks and astrological instruments dating from the reign of Rudolf II (14th century) testify to the high quality of Czech craftsmanship

in its heyday. There are also copies of the coronation seals, and an antique engraving depicting the execution of 27 Czech Protestant leaders that took place in 1621. An equally macabre sight is the sword allegedly used by the executioner, Mydlář. Since 1997 the so-called St Eligius treasure has been exhibited here, the most valuable piece being the mitre of Bishop Eligius († 660). Eight further gems belong to the treasure, including a sumptuous shrine and a cross decorated with precious jewels and pearls. *Daily except Monday, 9 am–5 pm; Metro: Hradčanská (A)*

House of the Black Madonna (U černé matky Boží) (109/D2)

★ Architect Josef Gočár erected this beautiful Cubist building in 1911 on the site where a Baroque house had previously stood. The original 17th-century house sign of the Black Madonna has been integrated into the new façade. Inside is the Czech Museum of Fine Arts. The top two floors feature a permanent exhibition of Czech Cubist art. *Daily except Mon. 10 am–6 pm; Celetná 34; Metro: Náměstí Republiky (B)*

Jewish Museum in Prague (Židovské muzeum u Praze) (108/C1)

★ ☆ By the 10th century, a community of Jewish merchants and traders were firmly settled in Prague. Their homes were clustered around what is now known as the Old-New Synagogue. Scientific and cultural life blossomed within the community, particularly during the 16th and 17th centuries. In the 19th century this ghetto became known as Josefov, named after Emperor Joseph II, who exercised tolerance towards what was by this time a significant Jewish population. Then tragically, in 1893, the area was completely 'rehabilitated' and the Jews were forced to move on. Only a few historically significant monuments were left standing. During the Second World War the Nazis, whose regime annihilated 90% of the city's Jewish population, brought to Prague numerous cultural and religious artefacts taken from 153 exterminated religious communities in Bohemia and Moravia, with the aim of creating a 'Museum of an extinct race'. In so doing, they unwittingly laid the foundations for the State Jewish Museum, opened in 1950, that documents the culture and religion of the Jewish people. All that remains of the centre of old Prague are the cemeteries, synagogues, ceremonial hall and the Jewish Town Hall (which now houses a huge kosher restaurant) and the Old-New Synagogue (Staronová synagóga), the oldest synagogue in Europe still in use and one of the oldest Gothic edifices in Prague. It is thought to have been built by Franciscan monks in around 1280. The tympanum was hewn from a single stone and portrays a vine (the tree of life) with twelve roots symbolizing the twelve tribes of Israel. A large flag hangs from the vaulting. This was a gift from Ferdinand II in recognition of the bravery displayed by the Jews during the battle against the Swedes in 1648. The pulpit is divided by a Gothic wrought-iron grille. Only men are allowed to pray in the main area; the gal-

leries are reserved for women. During services, the honorary chair that once belonged to the revered Rabbi Löw remains unoccupied. The Great Synagogue (or Jubilee Synagogue) is not in the former ghetto but in Jeruzalémská ulice (**109/F3**) and was built in 1906 in the Moorish style. In contrast to the Old-New synagogue, here the entire congregation is seated in the main hall during services. Since 1995, a festival of Jewish culture has been held here (May to October). The Klausen Synagogue (Klausova synagóga) is a Baroque hall building (1694). Opened recently here in the synagogue is the, to date, best and most extensive exhibition of 'Jewish Traditions and Customs – a Cycle of Life'. It is arranged according to individual themes, and encompasses Jewish holidays, weddings and prayers. The walls of the 11th century Pinkas Synagogue (Pinkasova synagóga) are inscribed with the names of the 77,297 Czech Jews killed in concentration camps. Children's drawings from the Theresiestadt concentration camp are also exhibited on the first floor. The Maisl synagogue (Maislova synagóga) was founded and financed by Mordechai Maisl, the wealthiest and most influential man in King Rudolph's Prague, in 1590-92 (or 5350-53 according to the Jewish calender). On the ground floor, an exhibit entitled 'The History of the Jews in Bohemia and Moravia' covers the period between the 10th and 18th centuries and features religious objects, crowns, lamps, and goblets. A depiction of Jewish history from the 18th century to 1945 in the Spanish Synagogue is to be seen in the Dušní ulice. The Ceremonial Hall (Obřadní síň) is part of the old Jewish cemetery. Since 1998 the exhibition 'Jewish Tradions and Customs – Funeral Brotherhood' can be seen here. *All buildings open daily except Sat., 9.30 am–7 pm; Old-New Synagogue 9 am–6 pm, Maiselova, Tel: 231 03 02 and 231 71 91, reservations for guides and groups; Metro: Staroměstká (A)*

Franz Kafka Museum (108/C2)

Since summer 1991, the Kafka Society has maintained a small museum in a modern building on the site where the writer's family home once stood. Exhibitions render an impression of the author's life and work through photographs and quotations. *Tues. to Sat. 10 am–6 pm; U radnice 5, Metro: Staroměstská (A)*

Mucha Museum
(Muchovo muzeum) (109/E3)

The Moravian painter Alfons Mucha (1860–1939) adopted in France the style of the day with decoratives lines in the Art Nouveau style. He achieved almost immediate fame for his poster for Sarah Bernhardt. There are around 80 of Mucha's works in the museum which was opened in 1998. *Palais Kaunický, Panská 7, Metro: Můstek (A)*

Museum of the City of Prague
(Muzeum hlavního města
Prahy) (103/D5)

The museum documents the history of Prague and the lives of its inhabitants. The main attraction is Antonín Langweil's model of the city, constructed between 1826 and 1837. The huge card-

board model shows the town centre as it was 150 years ago. *Daily except Mon. 10 am–6 pm; Karlín, Na poříčí 52, Metro: Florenc (B und C)*

Museum of Bohemian Glass
(Muzeum českého skla) (108/C2)

The museum shows the history of glass production in Bohemia from the 14th to the 20th century and a glass works in operation. *Daily except Mon. 10 am–9 pm, Staroměstské náměstí 26 (opposite the Town Hall), Metro: Můstek (A and B)*

Museum of Military History
(Vojenské muzeum) (101/D5)

This museum is situated near the Castle, inside one of Prague's most beautiful Renaissance structures. The façade of Schwarzenberg Palace features a geometric black and white sgraffito pattern in the Florentine style (1545-63). A large exhibition is dedicated to the Thirty Years War. In the courtyard are some historic cannons and other artil-

*Old field weapons:
the Military Museum*

lery of Austro-Hungarian and Prussian provenance. *May–Oct. daily except Mon. 10 am–6 pm; Hradčanské náměstí 2, Metro: Hradčanská (A)*

National gallery (Národní galerie)   (101/D5)

🚶 This palace was built by D. Martinelli and G. B. Alliprandi for Archbishop Šternberk. Most strongly represented are Dutch, German and Italian artists. Of the Dutch pieces dating from the 14th to 16th centuries, the most notable are the *Madonna with St Luke* by Jan Gossaert, known as Mabuse, and the major landscape *Haymaking* by Pieter Breughel the Elder, which is shown alongside a series painted by Breughel the Younger. Two altar paintings by Peter Paul Rubens, a painting by Franz Hals and an early Rembrandt, *The Old Scholar*, are the highlights among the 17th-century Flemish pieces. There are works by German painters ranging from the 14th to 18th centuries; the most significant of these is the *Feast of the Rosary* by Albrecht Dürer. Emperor Rudolf II purchased the picture for the gigantic sum of 20,000 Guilders and had it carried on poles over the Alps to Prague by alternating bearers. Two altar paintings by Holbein the Elder, *Portrait of an Old Man* by Cranach the Elder and works by Albrecht Altdorfer are also displayed. In addition to the 14th- and 15th-century paintings, the 16th- to 18th-century Italian collection (Tintoretto, Veronese) is worth seeing. Spanish art is represented by El Greco's *Head of Christ* and Goya's *Don Miguel Larzibadal.*

There is also a fine collection of Russian icons. Though none of the artists featured in the 20th-century art collection are actually Czech-born, it includes impressive works by Gustav Klimt (*Virgins*) as well as Egon Schiele, Oskar Kokoschka and Edvard Munch. Take some time to linger in the French art section, which features paintings by all the well-known masters from the Impressionist movement onwards (e.g. Monet, Cezanne, Van Gogh, Gauguin, Toulouse-Lautrec, Dufy and Matisse), as well as some early Picassos and sculptures by Rodin. Picnics are permitted in the gardens.
Daily except Mon. 10 am–6 pm; Hradčanské náměstí 15, Metro: Hradčanská (A)

National Museum (Národní muzeum)   (109/E5)

The monumental neo-Renaissance building that houses this museum — which has a 70 m (235ft) dome — was built by the Czech Josef Schulz in 1890, as a symbol of national rebirth. The allegorical figures on the parapet represent Bohemia; the Elbe is depicted as an old man, the Vltava as a virgin. The museum is organized in two separate sections, covering history and archeology. A tour of Europe's largest collection of minerals is highly recommended (an exceptional 40-carat diamond is one of the exhibit's highlights). There is an impressive collection of coins and medals dating back to the Přemyslid dynasty. The library contains one million volumes and 8000 manuscripts, including some priceless examples from the Middle Ages. *Daily 10 am–*

6 pm, Wed. 10 am–9 pm, Václavské náměstí, Metro: Muzeum (A und C)

Postage Museum (Poštovní muzeum) (109/E1)
★ Not even the staff dare estimate the number of postage stamps assembled here. The most valuable items on display include the world's first stamp, the *Penny Black* from England, the *Blue Mercury* stamp block and a collection of first stamps from all the countries of Europe. *Daily except Mon. 9 am–4.30 pm, Nové mlýny 2, Metro: Náměstí Republiky (B)*

Museum of Modern Art – National Gallery (Sbírka moderního umění – Národní galerie) (102/C3)
★ This building is a masterpiece of the Czech functionalist movement, and was designed by Oldřich Tyl and Josef Fuchs and built between 1924 and 1928 for the Prague Trade Fair. Le Corbusier marvelled at the construction, which confirmed that his own nascent plans for the League of Nations Palace in Geneva were indeed practicable. Following extensive renovations, the palace reopened in 1995 as Museum of Modern Art, showing European art of the 20th century, the famous collection of French art of the 19th and 20th centuries, and Czech art of the 20th century. Especially worth seeing are Czech artists such as Mucha, Kadář, Šíma, Toyen, Kupka, Štýrský, Filla, Šimotová, the Janoušeks, Kolíbal and Gutfreund. The collection of French art is the most extensive outside France, Russia and the United States. A number of Impressionist paintings are exhibited here, including works by Pissaro, Renoir, Toulouse-Lautrec, Gauguin and Van Gogh. There is an impressive range of paintings by Sisley, Monet, Cézanne, Seurat, Rousseau and Matisse. The exhibition also features no less than 19 Picassos, dating mostly from the period between 1906 and 1913. Braque, Chagall, Le Corbusier and Léger complete the collection. Norwegian artist Edvard Munch, whose *Dance at the Seaside* is shown here, was particularly influential on Czech art after his Prague exhibition of 1905. *Daily except Mon. 10 am–6 pm, Letná, Dukelských Hrdinů 47, Metro: Vltavská (C), trams 5, 12 und 17*

Smetana Museum (108/B3)
★ ⁂ ✝ Not very far from the Charles Bridge, on the banks of the Vltava, stands the Smetana Museum, named after Bedřich Smetana (1824-94), the father of Czech national music. Shown in the museum are letters, photographs, manuscripts of Smetana's compositions and some of his personal effects, such as his piano and also 19th century costumes from Smetana's operas. Tour the museum to strains of Smetana's *Vltava* and accompanied by the soft sounds of the Vlatva flowing past. *Novotného lávka, Metro: Staroměstská (A)*

Strahov Monastery (Strahovský klášter) (101/D5)
★ ⁂ The Strahov monastery was founded in 1140 by Prince Vladislav II, making it the second oldest in Prague. It rapidly developed into the centre of intellectual life. As the monastery was severely damaged by French bom-

A place for reflection and study: the library in Strahov Monastery

bardment in the year 1741, the present-day structure dates largely from the 17th and 18th centuries. Its library is one of the most celebrated sights in Prague. The *Strahov Evangeliar* is a valuable codex that was made in Trier in 860–865. The Theological Hall on the first floor, built from1671 to 1679 by Giovanni Domenico Orsi, is lined with Baroque bookcases – the display cabinets above the doors are for 'libri prohibiti'. At the centre of the room are geographical and astrological globes. The frescoes on the ceilings were painted by the monk Siardus Nosecký. One hundred years later, at the time of the French philosophical school known as the Encyclopaedists, the Philosophical Hall was built. It contains richly carved bookcases and a ceiling fresco, *The History of Philosophy*, created by Franz Anton Maulpertsch, in 1794. The south side-chapel of the Church of the Assumption of the Virgin contains the remains of Marshal von Pappenheim. *Daily except Mon. 9–12 am and 1–5 pm; Strahovské nádvoří 132: Metro: Hradčanská (A).*

Technical Museum (Národní technické muzeum) (102/B3)

★ ☆ This exhibition serves to remind the visitors that, until the Second World War, Czechoslovakia was among the world's foremost industrial nations. In the central hall stand the *Prezident* (1897), built in the Koprivnice Factory (now: Tatra), the 12-cylinder *Tatra* (1935) with a maximum speed of 140 km/h, and the lightweight *Voituretta* (1906) from the firm of Laurin and Klement, the forerunner of today's Škoda works. Especially valuable are the oldest Bugatti racing car and the oldest Audi, both from the year 1910. There are a total of 40 cars and 17 aircraft exhibited in the large hall. *Daily except Mon. 9 am–5 pm; Kostelní 42, Metro: Vltavská (C), trams 1 and 25*

Wax Museum

Two cabinets were opened in the year 1997: the *Prague Wax Museum* (109/D3), *28. října 13, Metro: Můstek (A)*, and the *Prague Panoptikum* (108/C4), *Národní 25, Metro: Národní třída (B); both are open daily from 10 am–20 pm.*

Where shall we eat?

Prague's famous wine restaurants – the Vinárna – have been serving excellent wine and culinary specialities for centuries

Just before sending him off to the guillotine, Robespierre reproached the gourmet Danton before the revolutionary tribunal with the assertion that his penchant for copious eating and drinking, Danton's renowned 'excesses', only served to compound his other offences. Likewise, when the country was in the grip of 'real socialism', visions of a rosy future were presented to the people, but the reality remained puritanical, grey and dreary. Czech culinary culture was repressed by the communist regime and it wasn't until the aftermath of the Velvet Revolution and the country's belated opening to tourism that gastronomic monotony and culinary stagnation were banished for good. This explains why our knowledge of traditional Bohemian cuisine tends to be limited to dumplings and pickles. Our expectations are not high, and we can only be pleasantly surprised

to discover that there is a real Czech cuisine, which is both substantial and flavourful.

In the better restaurants, the high demands of the guests are addressed, offering an ambiance that is cultivated, elegant and refined – as it is in the Hotel *Hoffmeister.* One can enjoy an exclusive ambiance and food in *Parnas.* At *U mecenáše*, Mr Koubek delights in guiding his customers through a veritable gastronomic labyrinth. There are also numerous restaurants specializing in wild game dishes: the chefs at *Myslivana* and *U Vladaře* prepare pheasant, venison and wild boar (and even bear!) to please the most discriminating of palates. Good quality, good value may be found at *Česká hospoda*, in *U Jindřišské věže*, in *Klub novinářů* and in *Gany's.*

Since the Velvet Revolution of 1989, most restaurants in Prague have become privately owned, and, as a consequence, culinary standards have risen. The political changes the country has undergone have spilled over into the gastronomic realm, and new eateries are springing up like mushrooms.

In a beer garden rich in tradition, such as U Fleků , the citizens of Prague enjoy a cool beer

The typical Czech dining experience starts off with the popular aperitif, *Becherovka*, a slightly bitter red-currant liqueur from Karlovy Vary, which is served with ice, a lemon wedge and sometimes tonic. The composition of the already more than 190-year-old trademake is known to only two people in the world. The liqueur comprises twenty medicinal herbs and spices. That means that pure health is swishing around in the bottle, and perhaps that is the reason the *Becherovka* is known as the 'thirteenth Karlsbad Spa'. The latest hit among the aperitifs is Fernet with tonic, also known as *Bavorák* (Bavarian). A shot of *Fernet* neat, by the way, is known as 'the touch of the dead lover'. In some restaurants one can treat oneself to a special entrée – real Russian caviar, sometimes accompanied by a glass of ice-cold vodka. Often, the customer is presented with a trolley piled with hot and cold hors d'œuvres to choose from.

When it comes to main courses, the selection is even more vast. Some classic choices include *svíčková na smetaně* (roast beef in a delicate bittersweet cream sauce with dumplings), *vepřová pečeně se zelím* (roast pork with cabbage) or *pečená husa* (roast goose). In addition to the usual potatoes and dumplings, new side dishes have begun to appear, such as *bramborák*, a kind of potato fritter with garlic and marjoram that is a perfect accompaniment for the wide array of meat dishes on offer. To satisfy the guest's eye and palate, waiters will often flambé some of the main courses in vodka, gin or cognac at the table. A digestif is a memorable experience, and not just for the stomach. Cognac is served in one of the 'Giant Snifters' from the celebrated Moser glass factory at Karlovy Vary. Depending on the physiognomy of the guest, the waiter selects an appropriate glass – they all have names such as Long Face, Moon Face, Long Fellow, Stout Gentleman, Slim Lady and Big Bertha! In restaurants such as *U mecenáše*, the waiter will put on a real show, juggling the filled glass over the flames which he then extinguishes with a magician's flourish.

In Prague it is not customary to have cheese at the end of a meal, as the choices are limited and the quality is inconsistent. Likewise, fresh salads are a rarity out of season. However, desserts (*moučníky*) are another matter entirely – menus are filled with mouthwatering sweets such as *palačinky*, *lívanec*, *dort* and *buchta*; pastries stuffed with plums, raspberries or cherries and served with fromage blanc sprinkled with poppy seeds; caramel flambéed fruit and refined ice creams.

For many years, a war over who brews the best beer has been raging amongst Prague's 900 pubs. Real beer aficionados swear by the prestigious Pilsner Urquell or Pilsner Gambrinus (the 1993 beer of the year), Budvar, Radegast (the beer of 1994), Krušovice, Rakovnik, Staropramen, Bráník, Platan, Regent, and Pragovar. Those who love dark beers, will choose Purkmistr from Pilsen, or Fleksche beer from the brewery of the same name, with 13% original wort.

Westerners consider the first five of the series to be the best. In the restaurant *Gany's* one can also drink the best beer of the year 1996, Radegast, in the restaurant *Skorepka* Gambrinus, the beer of the year 1997. Competition is constant between hundreds of pubs (specifically their land-lords), over the most skillfully poured Pilsner Urquell. The freshest, smoothest Pilsner is poured at *U zlatého tygra*. Another favourite is *U kalicha*, the walls of which are decorated with sayings and engravings re-counting the story of the brave soldier Schwejk (it was here that he wanted to meet Sappeur Vodička 'at six o'clock after the war').

When it comes to atmosphere and romance, the centuries-old taverns and stylish wine bars tucked away in the Baroque houses of the old town and Malá Strana have plenty of both. A speciality of the Old Town are the establishments in the Gothic cellars, in what was the ground floors 600 years ago. During the 17th century, the streets and squares were raised by one level in an effort to reduce the damage from flooding, so guests entering a 17th-century Baroque house need only descend a staircase to find themselves immersed in a 14th-century setting. Gothic and Romanesque ground floors have since become the cellars of pop-ular establishments such as the *U pavouka*, *U kamenného stolu*, *U zlaté studně* and *Flambée*.

Less intimate and more mod-ern are the city's many snack bars and bistros, where bufets are comprised of a sandwich and a cheap glass of wine and the ubiq-uitous automats serve a wine *du jour* to accompany very reason-ably priced food. There are also a number of stands where at any time of day you can purchase a

MARCO POLO SELECTION: RESTAURANTS

1 Česká hospoda
Pleasant place. Suitable for a small wallet (page 60)

2 Circle Line Brasserie
Utterly French – except the service (page 55)

3 Gany's
Cuisine for the calory conscious (page 58)

4 Lobkovická vinárna
A princely wine bar in the Little Quarter (page 57)

5 Myslivna
Game specialities (page 58)

6 Parnas
Terrific food, beautiful view (page 56)

7 U Jindřišské věže
Eating and drinking at civilised prices (page 62)

8 U modré kachničky
Where Chancellor Kohl and Václav Havel dined (page 57)

9 U Vladaře
Cooking as fine art (page 58)

10 Valdštejnská hospoda
Varied menu in an old establishment (page 59)

small pitcher of wine to wash down a hot sausage smothered in mustard. Tourists, who are generally surprised at this surfeit of choice, have recently dubbed Wenceslas Square 'the stomach of Prague'. Unlike the restaurants, which have recovered nicely from the hardships of the socialist regime, Prague's cafés (*kavárna*) remain relatively morose and anonymous – sometimes even downright shabby. It is hard to imagine that, during the period prior to the Second World War, these places were important cultural centres frequented by artists and journalists who would come to read local and foreign newspapers and chat over a cup of coffee. Two classics in the category of Art Nouveau cafés have recently been radiantly restored: the *Slavi*, the café of writers and poets, in which Smetana used to compose, and the *Café in the House of Representation*. During the 1920s, Kafka, Brod, Kisch and Werfel, among others, would gather regularly at the *Arco*. This old and honourable café was, unfortunately, closed some years ago.

One of the few cafés that has managed to preserve its original Art Nouveau setting and the charms of a bygone era is the beautiful *Evropa* café on Wenceslas Square.

However, in not all of Prague's establishments is the service, unfortunately, friendly and honest. This is especially true for such restaurants in which a frequent flow of tourists is seen.

CAFÉS

T = Terrace

Amadeus   (108/C2)
Eighty years ago, Einstein used to play the violin on the first floor of the 'House with the Stone Table'. Today, the Café Amadeus offers visitors to Prague a pleasant view of the Staroměstské náměstí. Expensive. *Daily 8 am–8 pm; Staroměstské náměstí 18, Metro: Můstek (A und B)*

Bílý jelínek (T)
(The White Stag)   (108/C2)
⚐ This café is located in a Baroque house behind the Old Town Hall, opposite the house where Franz Kafka was born. In fine weather, you can have your coffee and cakes under the umbrellas on the terrace and watch the world go by. *Daily 10 am–12 pm; U radnice 12 am– 2 pm; Metro: Staroměstská (A)*

Four-hundred Millers

Some people may be surprised that one encounters so many German names among the artists of Prague. The long centuries of the Czechs and the Germans living so closely together led to many people Bohemianising or Germanising their names. One thus finds in Germany or in Vienna names like Nowak, Prochaska, and Vranitzky, and in the Prague telephone book, four-hundred times Müller and Müllerová. Schwejk's charlady was also named Müllerová.

Café-Bar (T) (108/C2)

In the Renaissance house on the Staromestské námestí, fine sgraffitos show scenes from ancient mythology. Franz Kafka spent much of his childhood here. 30 different kinds of tea and coffee. *Daily 10 am–11 pm; Staroměstské náměstí 3/2, Metro: Staroměstská (A)*

Café de Paris (109/E2)

Located in a Neo-Gothic building (1904) with Art Nouveau elements, this pleasant café has a wide selection of coffees and cakes. *Daily 6.30 am–1 am; U obecního domu 1, Metro: Náměstí Republiky (B)*

Café Poet (T) (101/D5)

Comfortable café and restaurant situated to the left of the main entrance to Prague Castle. *Daily 9 am–8 pm; Metro: Hradčanská (A)*

Evropa (T) (109/E4)

An absolute treat for lovers of Art Nouveau and highly recommended. The café boasts original lamps and chandeliers; countless murals and mirrors decorate the interior. The lovely horseshoe balcony has only recently been reopened. *Daily 7 am–12 pm; Live Music Wed–Sun, 3 am–12 pm; Václavské náměstí 29, Metro: Můstek (A und B)*

A well-earned pause when walking in the Old Town

Gany's (108/C4)

♣ Thirties Art Deco café with seven billiard tables in two rooms, a room for non-smokers, English and German papers, Radegast beer, several kinds of coffee, breakfast around 50 Kč. Sensible prices. *Daily 8 am–11 pm; Národní 20, Metro: Národní třída (B)*

The Globe (102/C3)

♣ The uninhibited relaxed atmosphere of the New World – from where the owner also comes – flows through this room. It is very popular with young tourists. Mostly English literature is available at the bookshop attached. *Daily 10 am–12 pm; Janovského 24, Metro: Vltavská (C)*

Kajetánka (T) (101/E5)

◁▷ Directly beneath the castle approach, located in the former Church of St Mary. The café has a terrace with a great view of the Little Quarter, the Strahov Monastery and the Old Town. *Daily 11 am–8 pm, in winter 11am–6 pm; Kajetánské zahrady, Metro: Hradčanská (A)*

Malostranská kavárna (T)
(Little Quarter Café) (101/E5)

Located in the Rococo house 'The Stone Table' – this old (1874) and traditional artists' café has recently been re-opened after many years of being closed. A number of well-known Czech and German *literati* – such as Max Brod, Franz Werfel, Egon Erwin Kisch und Karl Čapek – used to meet here. And when one is sitting in this café, one has the impression that their ghosts are still present here today. *Malostranské náměstí 28, Metro: Malostranská (A)*

Milena (108/C2)

This venue is named after one of Kafka's lovers, Milena Jesenská (*Letters to Milena*). The Prague journalist and restistance fighter died in 1944 in a concentration camp. The café is housed in the Franz Kafka Society building, opposite the Old Town Hall, and was designed in 1920s style. Great live piano music. *Daily 10 am–10 pm; Staroměstské náměstí 22, Metro: Staroměstská (A)*

Repre Café (109/E2)

Sumptuously ornamental Art Nouveau, plus a fountain of light, makes for a good atmosphere – live piano music in the background after 6 pm. *Daily 7.30 am–11 pm; Náměstí Republiky (Metro line B)*

Slavia (108/B4)

◁▷ ✿ This historic café (1863) just opposite the National Theatre was a meeting place for musicians such as Bedřich Smetana, writers like Karel Čapek and Nobel prize winner Jaroslav Seifert. From the large window looking over the Vltava and Hradcany, Rainer Maria Rilke composed his poetic declaration of love to Czech Prague, *Larenopfer*. Renovated in Art Deco style, the café was symbolically reopened on the anniversary of the Velvet Revolution, November 17, 1997. *Daily 8 am–12 pm; Národní 1, Metro: Národní třída (B)*

U bakaláře (109/D2)

♣ A student café in the city centre, with cheap food and drink. Also a good place for breakfast. *Mo–Fr 8.30 am–7 pm; Sat and Sun 1–7 pm; Celetná 13, Metro: Náměstí Republiky (B)*

A place with history and tales: for over 100 years artists and poets have met at the Café Slavia

U mostecké věže (101/E5)
Located by the bridge tower, on the site occupied by the Swedes during the siege of the Little Quarter in 1648. Today, the same spot is invaded by tourists of every nationality. Snacks, beer, wine and coffee. *Daily 10 am–12 pm; Mostecká 3, Metro: Malostranská (A)*

U Týna (T) (109/D2)
Beneath the Gothic arch in front of the Týn Church. From the café terrace, you can hear the bells of the astronomical clock chiming the hour. A good place to enjoy a glass of wine. *Daily 10 am–10 pm; Staroměstské náměstí 15, Metro: Můstek (A und B)*

Velryba (108/C4)
☂ This simple and reasonably priced café is located in the centre of Prague, and it is popular mainly with the students. *Daily 11 am–2 am, Opatovická 24, Metro: Národní třída (B)*

RESTAURANTS

Category 1
Meal for one person including wine, 600–1000 Kč

Čertovka (T) (108/A2)
☃ Tucked away on the banks of the river – you can gain access to this restaurant via a narrow staircase. Nice view of the Old Town. *Daily 11am–11 pm; U lužického semináře 24, Tel: 53 88 53, Metro: Malostranská (A)*

Circle Line Brasserie (101/E5)
★ According to the Prague Gourmet guide, this restaurant is in first place, certainly because the kitchen chef is French. In the lovely milieu of the Little Quarter, directly opposite the Church of St Niklas. French cuisine, French and Moravian wines, attentive service. *Daily except Sun 6–11 pm; Malostranské náměstí 12, Tel: 53 03 08, Metro: Malostranská (A), trams 12 und 22*

The Gourmet Palaces of Prague

Club Restaurant (109/E3)
The Hotel Palace offers Bohemian and international cuisine in a restaurant with with a combination of Art Nouveau and Art Deco styles. From 1000 Kč. *Daily 6–11 pm; Panská 12, Tel: 24 09 31 11, Metro: Můstek (A and B)*

Hoffmeister (101/F5)
One dines here surrounded by original drawings by the father of the owner. In an extensively furnished room one enjoys the cuisine of old Bohemia and French specialities. A good choice of wines. From 1000 Kč. *Daily 12 am–11 pm; Pod Bruskou 9, Tel: 57 31 09 42, Metro: Malostranská (A)*

Opera Grill (108/B4)
In a small stylishly furnished room – with a capacity of only two dozen guests – one can sit comfortably in the airmchairs and chat with the owner. One senses a whiff of luxury everywhere. The chef is proud of his duck with *Bramborák*. Good white wines from Žernoseky, the Ruländer comes from Roudnice. From 1000 Kč. *Daily 7 pm–2 am; Karoliny Světlé 35, Tel: 26 55 08, Metro: Staroměstská (A)*

Parnas (108/B4)
★ ⬧ Beautiful view of the Hradschin and Charles Bridge. Delicate Norwegian and Canadian fish specialities, and good international cuisine. One feels at ease in the room with inlaid precious wood, green marble and a magnificent, long bar. From 1200 Kč. *Daily 12 am–3 pm and 6–12 pm; from 8 pm live piano music, Smetanovo nábřeží 2, Tel: 24 21 19 01, Metro: Národní třída (B)*

U mecenáše
(The Patron) (101/E5)
A top establishment with a history. In the first is what is assumed to be the little table of the Prague hangman from 1634, in the second room sit the guests of prominence. Best Bohemian cuisine, good wines and, morever, the perfectly friendly service of Mr Koubek. 500–900 Kč. *Daily 12 am–11.30 pm; Malostranské náměstí 10, Tel: 53 38 81, Metro: Malostranská (A)*

U zlaté hrušky
(The Golden Pear) (101/D5)
This luxury restaurant is in the picturesque lane, Nový svět. Stylish interior, agreeable ambience, selected specialities. A lovely garden-restaurant. Lunch menu 300 Kč, in the evening à la carte 1000 Kč. *Daily 11.30 am–3 pm and 6.30–12 pm; Nový svět 3, Tel: 20 51 47 78, Metro: Hradčanská (A)*

V zátiší (108/B3)
The menu is irresistible: grilled crayfish with garlic sauce as an entrée and fish Wellington in a white wine sauce, with Moravian wine from Pavlovice or Chablis, expertly served. The leg of duck is also a speciality of the chef. Always full, table reservation an absolute must. From 700 Kč. *Daily 12 am–3 pm and 5.30–11 pm; Liliová 1, Tel: 24 22 89 77, Metro: Národní třída (B)*

Fakhreldine (102/C4)
This branch of the restaurant of the same name in London's Piccadilly Circus seems to have conjured up spirits like those of Aladdin in Arabia. Lebanese cuisine with lamb and chicken, Arabian desserts and wines. *Daily 12 am–11.30 pm; Klimentská 48, Tel: 232 79 70, Metro: Náměstí Republiky (B)*

John Bull (109/E2)
A typical English restaurant opposite the Powder Tower. English and Czech beer, and Bohemian steaks without mad-cow disease. *Daily 11 am–11 pm; Senovážná 8, Tel: 24 22 60 05, Metro: Náměstí Republiky (B)*

Lobkovická vinárna (101/D5)
★ Stylish and in keeping with the aristocratic tastes of the Little Quarter, this restaurant stands next to the German Embassy. It was built 100 years ago by Prince Lobkovicz. Good steaks and a good choice of Melnik wines that are offered by the descendent of the builder. *Daily 12 am–3 pm and 6.30–12 pm; Vlašská 17, Tel: 53 01 85, Metro: Malostranská (A)*

Nebozízek (T) (101/E6)
◁▷ Reached by cable car, this restaurant and café is perched on Petřín Hill, 100 m above the Vltava, and offers food that rivals the spectacular view. *Daily 11 am–6 pm and 7–11 pm; Petřínské sady, Tel: 53 79 05, Metro: Národní třída (B)*

La Provence (109/D2)
Top establishment with ambience, cuisine, champagne and wines à la Provence. The prices are accordingly for crevettes, coq au vin, Bœuf provençal or breast of duck in honey sauce. Extremely wide selection of French wines and cheeses. Unfortunately, too little room to eat. *Daily 12 am–1 am, Štupartská 9, Tel: 232 48 01, Metro: Náměstí Republiky (B)*

Tosca (101/D5)
This very good restaurant is in the old Palace Toskánský near the castle. Cuisine from Tuscany and Bohemia. Evergreen Night Club in the evening with music and dancing. *Restaurant daily 10 am–10 pm, Wine bar 12 am–3 pm and 6 pm–1 am; Hradčanské náměstí 5, Tel: 53 18 97, Metro: Hradčanská (A)*

U modré kachničky
(The Blue Duck) (101/E6)
★ Chancellor Kohl dined with Václav Havel in this colorful restaurant. Old Bohemian cuisine. Nine different duck dishes. *Daily 12 am–3 pm and 6.30–11 pm; Nebovidská 6, Tel: 57 32 03 08, Metro: Malostranská (A), trams 12 and 22*

U pavouka (The Spider) (109/D2)
You enter a Baroque house of 18th century, walk down 32 steps and take a surprising leap into the Gothic. A walled-up Gothic window in the cellar leads from that epoch straight on to the street. *Daily noon to midnight, Celetná 17, Tel: 24 81 14 36, Metro: Můstek (A und B)*

U staré synagogy
(The Old Synagogue) (108/C1)
On the menu of this luxury restaurant near the old new synagogue are specialities of old Bo-

hemian cuisine. Enjoy the lovely Art Nouveau atmosphere with live piano music. *Daily 11.30 am–12 pm; Pařížská 17, Tel: 231 85 52, Metro: Staroměstská (A)*

U Vladaře (101/E6)
★ This cosy restaurant in an old house offers the dishes of old Prague and game specialities. Good wines from Zernoseky and Moravia. *Daily 11 am–1 am, Maltézské náměstí 10, Tel: 53 81 28, Metro: Malostranská (A)*

Category 2
Meal for one person including wine, from 300 Kč

Gany's (108/C4)
★ Cuisine for the calorie-conscious, with a choice of four salads all the year round (which is still something of a rarity in Prague). Vegetarian meals, fish, chicken. Reasonable prices. *Daily 11 am–11 pm; Národní 20, 2nd floor, Tel: 29 76 65, Metro: Národní třída (B)*

James Joyce Irish Pub (108/B3)
⚐ A piece of Ireland in Prague. Only the cook speaks Czech. But his Molly Bloom's Irish Steak is still fabulous and without BSE. Vegetarian breakfast and, moreover, Joyce's Late Breakfast will fill you up for the rest of the day. Irish whiskey, Irish and Czech beers. *Daily 10.30 am–1 am; Liliová 10, Tel: 24 22 19 83, Metro: Národní třída (B)*

Košer restaurace Shalom (Kosher Restaurant) (108/C1)
Guests come from all over the world to this restaurant with its unusual ambience. *Daily 11.30 am–2 pm; Friday dinner after the* service at the synagogue, Maislova 18, Tel: 24 81 09 29, Metro: Staroměstská (A)

Letenský zámeček (Letná Castlets) (102/B4)
Opposite the Technical Museum is the second oldest carousel in the world. A few steps further on are the three restaurants of the Letenský zámeček. The garden restaurant offers traditional Bohemian cuisine and good Kozel beer at reasonable prices. The prices and food in the restaurant *Ullmann* are similar, while next door in the restaurant *Belcredi* a good meal costs 200–400 Kč. You can have coffee or a cognac in the small room in the castle tower, and enjoy a fine view. *Ullmann: daily 10 am–12 pm, Belcredi: daily 11 am–2 am, Tel: 37 12 06, Metro: Vltavská (C), trams 1 and 25*

Myslivna (Forester's Lodge) (107/E2)
★ Pheasant – 'food for the gods' according to Voltaire – wild duck, and other game served with bramborák potatoes. *Daily 12 am–4 pm and 5–12 pm; Jagelonská 21, Tel: 627 02 09, Metro: Flora (A)*

Oscar's (109/D2)
Theme restaurant with film designs on the walls. Program in the evening. Below the Renaissance Granovský Palace in the new Ungelt Centre behind the Týn Church. *Daily 11 am–12 pm; Týnský dvůr 639, Tel: 24 89 54 04, Metro: Můstek (A und B)*

Red Hot And Blues (109/D2)
American restaurant, Texas specialities, breakfast in the garden. *Daily 9 am–11 pm; Wed, Fri, Sat*

Golden Fountain (U zlaté studně)

(101/E5) High above the rooftops of the Little Quarter, just beneath the Castle, is this traditional terrace restaurant. After dark, the legendary hundred towers of Prague seem to be much closer from here, and the moon and the stars all seem within reach from here. One is almost tempted to pluck them and hang them on then spires like so many pretzels. The calm pervading this spot even affected the German and Czech students who, back in the days of growing nationalism, would sit here peacefully taking turns to sing their anthems, "Watch on the Rhine" and "Hej Slované".

Jazz, Sat and Sun Brunch, Jakubská 12, Tel: 231 46 39, Metro: Náměstí Republiky (B)

Restaurant Jan Paukert   (108/C4)
Intimate and elegant in the style of the thirties. Old Prague cuisine, quail, pheasant, roast goose with bread and potato dumplings. Wines from Žernoseky. *Daily 11.30 am–11 pm; Národní 17, Tel: 26 64 44, Metro: Národni třída (B)*

U Golema (The Golem)   (108/C1)
Immerse yourself in the atmosphere of this magical place where the Golem once caused havoc. A gilded sculpture of the mythical figure, created by Rabbi Löw, stands in the largest room. Try the 'Rabbi's Bag' (rabinova kapsa). *Mo–Fr 11 am–10 pm, Sat 5–11 pm, Maislova 8, Tel: 232 81 65, Metro: Staroměstská (A)*

U kamenného stolu (The Stone Table)   (109/D2)
In the rooms of the café on the first floor Albert Einstein explained his theory of relativity in 1910 to listeners such as Max Brod und Franz Kafka. Bohemian cuisine, day bar, own confectionary shop. *Daily 11 am–10 pm; Staroměstské náměstí 18, Tel: 24 21 20 26, Metro: Můstek (A und B)*

U pastýřky (The Shepherdess)   (106/C2)
Log cabin interior and traditional music, with good char-grilled meals and wine from the cask. Reservations recommended. *Daily 6 pm–1 am; Bělehradská 14, Tel: 43 43 19, Metro: I. P. Pavlova (C), trams 6 and 11*

U Plebána (The Parson)   (108/C3)
✸ Comfortable restaurant serving international cuisine and traditional Czech specialities. Reservations are necessary in the evening. *Daily from noon to midnight; Betlémské náměstí 10, Tel: 24 22 90 23, Metro: Národní třída (B)*

U zlaté studně (T) (Golden Spring)   (101/E5)
⤼ Enjoy the panorama over the city rooftops from the enchanting wine bar terrace, on the 5th floor of the hotel. *Daily 11 am–12pm; U zlaté studně 166, Metro: Malostranská (A)*

Valdštejnská hospoda (Waldstein Hostelry)   (101/E5)
★ This hostelry has little in common with General Waldstein

who shares its name. It actually lies near his palace. As in almost all of the streets in the Little Quarter, there is also a spook in Waldstein Square where a headless nightwatchman is making mischief. He used to blow very loudly beneath Waldstein's bedroom window every hour, until the general had him beheaded. Game, fish, beef and pork are offered on the richly varied menu at this lovely old restaurant. Bohemian and south Moravian wines. Booking in advance is absolutely required. *Daily 11.30 am–11.30 pm; Valdštejnské náměstí 7, Tel: 53 87 04; Metro: Malostranská (A)*

Vikárka (101/E5)

430 years ago the former vicar of St Vitus Cathedral received from the Archbishop the permission to give wine to not only the clergy, but also to normal citizens. Because President Václav Havel lives around the corner in Prague Castle, he is practically a regular. With the classic Bohemian

dishes with dumplings one drinks Staropramen beer. *Daily 11 am–12 pm; Vikářská 6, Tel: 24 51 06 86, Metro: Hradčanská (A)*

Znojemská vinárna (Znaimer Wine Cellar) (109/D3)

An elegant restaurant serving South Moravian specialities such as *Vranov* schnitzel. Round off your meal with pancakes. *Daily 11.30 am–11 pm; Václavské náměstí 7, Tel: 24 19 36 90, Metro: Můstek (A und B)*

Category 3

Meal for one person including wine or beer, from 100 Kč

Česká hospoda (Czech Hostelry) (109/E5)

★ Comfortable, clean restaurant, friendly service, good Bohemian cooking and fantastic beer. Crispy duck 105 Kč, Wienerschnitzel 101 Kč. Just 100m (330ft) from Wenceslas Square. *Daily 10 am–11 pm; Krakovská 20, Tel: 22 21 02 04, Metro: Museum (A and C)*

Wine and coffee to the hourly chimes of the Loreto Church

FOOD & DRINK

Evropa (109/E4)

⚓ The Pilsner restaurant in the basement of the Evropa Hotel is decorated in beautiful Art Nouveau style. The atmosphere is better than the conventional Bohemian cooking. They do serve good Pilsner on draught. *Daily 10 am–11 pm; Václavské náměstí 29, Tel: 24 22 81 17, Metro: Můstek (A und B)*

Jo's Bar (101/E5)

⚓ One sits under the arcades at the gigantic St Nikla Church, to eat Mexican or vegetarian food, and drink Czech beer in a Canadian bistro. *Daily 11 am–2 am, Sun Brunch, Malostranské náměstí 7, Tel: 53 12 51, Metro: Malostranská (A), trams 12 and 22*

Klub novinářů (Press Club) (108/C1)

A favourite watering hole for journalists and members of the press. The schnitzel in cheese sauce goes down well with a cool glass of Pilsner Urquell. Pleasingly low prices. *Daily 11 am–10 pm, Pařížská 9, Tel: 232 26 18, Metro: Staroměstská (A)*

Makarská (101/E5)

The wine bar on the Little Quarter Ring is more than 100 years old. Fish, game, chicken and Bohemian dishes in the heart of the Little Quarter. Steak for 200 Kč. The bar serves good South Moravian and French wines. *Daily noon to midnight; Malostranské náměstí 2, Tel: 53 13 18, Metro: Malostranská (A)*

Plzeňská Restaurace (Pilsner Restaurant) (109/E2)

The entire furnishings of this popular restaurant are straight Art Nouveau. The large ceramic mosaic *Bohemian Harvest* is from Jakub Obrovský. Old Bohemian cuisine, Pilsner Urquell. *Daily 10.30 am–11 pm; Náměstí Republiky, Tel: 22 00 27 80, Metro: Náměstí Republiky (B)*

Tři grácie (T) (The Three Graces) (108/B3)

〰 South Moravian specialities and wines from Mikulov. A stone's throw away from the historic Charles Bridge. Great view of the bridge from the terrace. Reservations are necessary during the peak season. *Daily 10 am–12 pm; Novotného lávka 5, Tel: 24 22 91 06, Metro: Staroměstská (A)*

U Fleků (T) Flek Brewery (108/C5)

⚓ ☼ The most famous bar in town has become a popular meeting place for tourists. Lager has been lovingly brewed here for 500 years, while the 13% proof dark beer, with its characteristic smoky caramel aftertaste, has been brewed here since 1843. In the Old Bohemian Hall hang pictures of the 'greatest' Czech painter, the two-meter (6"3') Láčla Novák, also known as 'Ladislaus Longinus'. The tragic theme of one of his pictures is *The Last Beer*. One can try the speciality of the house here, *pivní sýr a topinky* (beer cheese with roasted garlic bread), which is prepared for 900 guests, for which reason the waiter proffers the bill immediately. Be advised that the Becherovka aperitif offered, is not on the house! *Daily 9 am–11 pm (brass bands in summer); Křemencova 11, Tel: 24 91 51 18, Metro: Národní třída (B), from there it's another 600m (2000ft).*

Brewery and restaurant combined: a meeting place for beer lovers from all over the world

U Jindřišské věže
(At the Henry Tower) (109/E3)
★ ✆ The food is simple, tasty, and good value for money – the beer and wine, too. The service is attentive. Light and dark Měšťan beer. From 12 am to 1.30 pm, it is difficult to find a seat. *Daily 11 am–11.30 pm, Jindřišská 26, Tel: 24 23 02 26, Metro: Můstek (A, B)*

U kalicha (The Chalice) (106/C2)
‡ This beer restaurant is a tourist attraction. It played an important role twice in the life of Schwejk: he was arrested here by a secret policeman. And his famous words were: 'At six o'clock in the evening, after the war, at The Chalice.' Bohemian cuisine, Pils beer, dark Purkmistr beer and Radegast. Impolite service. *Daily 11 am–11 pm; brass band music from 7.30 pm, Na bojišti 12–14, Tel: 29 07 01, Metro: I. P. Pavlova (C)*

U malého Glena
(Little Glenn's) (101/E5)
Canadian restaurant offering breakfast, lunch, and dinner in a typical milieu. *Daily 9 am–3 am, featuring live jazz, reggae or acid music every evening; Karmelitská 23, Tel: 535 81 15, Metro: Malostranská (A), trams 12 and 22*

U Rudolfa
(The Rudolf) (108/C1)
✆ The smallest wine bar in Prague in the heart of the Jewish Old Town. Good food – try their 'Rabbi's Bag'. *Daily 10 am–10 pm, Maislova 5, Tel: 232 26 71, Metro: Staroměstská (A)*

U Schnellů (Schnell's) (101/E5)
In the middle of the aristocratic Little Quarter, this famous restaurant (founded 1784) has catered to such illustrious clients as Peter the Great as well as Saxon and Bavarian kings. Good Bohemian cooking. *Daily 11 am–12 pm, Tomášská 2, Tel: 53 20 04, Metro: Malostranská (A)*

U supa (The Vulture) (109/D2)
During the Middle Ages, many restaurants lined Celetná, which is the ancient passageway between the Old Town Market (Staroměstské náměstí) and the Powder Tower. This is one of the survivors, offering Bohemian food and the wonderful Krušovice beer. *Daily 11.30 am–11 pm; Celetná 22, Tel: 24 21 20 04, Metro: Můstek (A and B)*

PUBS

Černý kůň (Black Horse) (109/D4)
Radegast draught beer. *Daily 11 am–11 pm; Vodičkova 36*

Krušovická pivnice
(Krušovicer pub) (108/C1)
Named after the beer it has on tap (Krušovice), which is served with reasonably priced food. *Daily 11 am–12 pm; Široká 20*

Radegast (109/D2)
Simple pub with terrific Radegast beer and Bohemian cuisine. *Daily 11 am–12 pm; Templová, Celetná Passage 27*

Skořepka (108/C3)
Pilsner Urquell, Gambrinus, Purkmistr, and leg of pork. *Daily 11.30 am–10 pm; Skořepka 1*

U Bubeníčků
(Bubeníček's) (108/B5)
Sample the renowned Gambrinus beer from Plzen, along with traditional Bohemian cooking. *Mon–Fri 9 am–10 pm, Sat and Sun 11 am–9 pm; Myslíkova 6*

U Černého vola
(The Black Ox) (101/D5)
'The Black Ox' serves good Popovice beer on draught. *Daily 10 am–10 pm; Loretánská 2*

U dvou koček
(The Two Cats) (108/C3)
'The Two Cats' features Pilsner Urquell and a number of other surprising brews. Traditional Bohemian food. *Daily 11 am–11 pm; Uhelný trh 10*

U kocoura (The Tomcat) (101/E5)
'The Tomcat' serves Pilsner Urquell on draught. *Daily 11 am–11 pm; Nerudova 2*

U Pinkasů
(The Pinkas) (109/D4)
Pinkus the tailor acquired this hostelry and had the first barrel of beer from Pilsen brought here in 1843. It was in this way that the fame of the bitter Pilsner Urquell beer spread first in Prague, and then throught the world. *Daily 9 am–11 pm; Jungmannovo náměstí 15*

U svatého Tomáše
(The St Thomas) (101/E5)
The Augustine monks founded the brewery in 1358, For almost 600 years the clever monks brewed the black beer to the glory of God and their own profit, but there is now Braník beer here. Various dishes are grilled in the beer garden. The waiters, unfortunately, are rather unfriendly. *Daily 11.30 am–12 pm; brass band music in the tourist season from 8–12 pm; Letenská ulice 12*

U Vejvodů
(Vejvoda's Pub) (108/C3)
Staropramen beer. Great Bohemian dishes on the menu, which are also good value. *Daily 10 am–11 pm; Jilská 4*

U zlatého tygra
(The Golden Tiger) (108/C3)
Above the entrance is depicted a tiger – with a strange leg position, however. Be that as it may – this is the place to sample the best Pilsner Urquell on draught, which Presidents Clinton and Havel enjoyed together in 1994. The most prominent guest, however, at least until his death, was the famous writer Bohumil Hrabral. To the right of the entrance to this pub hangs a painting depicting him as a gentle barbarian, along with a tigress. *Daily 3 am–10.30 pm; Husova 17*

A shopper's paradise

On the Golden Cross, you can buy Bohemian glass, dark-red garnets, chic fashions, antiques and traditional art

With the exchange rate at around 50 Kč to the pound sterling, and 30 Kč to the dollar (January 1999 rates), there is shopping at reasonable prices to be found in Prague. The most important shopping centre is the so-called Golden Cross, an elegant pedestrian precinct around Wenceslas Square, Na příkopě, ulice 28 října, and Národní třída. In the lanes nearby one finds good and very often fine stores where one can buy the famous Bohemian crystal, jewellery made from dark-red Bohemian garnet, antiques, modern tapestry, objets d'art, LPs and CDs of classical music, as well as coffee-table books in various languages and sundry souvenirs of Prague. Fashionable clothes, elegant hats, handbags and cheap leather goods can also be found. There are chic collections of fashions to be found everywhere, such as those from Daniel Hechter in the Wenceslas Passage, or Boss suits on Jungmannova náměstí. The select fashion house in the Palace Versace in the Celetná is worth a visit, although a hand-painted man's shirt costs no less than 25,000 Kč – but there are only eight of them in the world. The extreme diversity on show in the windows of the many antique shops are a real feast for the eyes – you can find excellent glass and filigree work. A visit to the Moser Glass Company ('The Glass of Kings, The King of Glass') is well worth the time – if only to admire its wooden walls with fine marquetry and the valuable, hundred-year-old glass windows. In the better hotels there are also small shops with glass, porcelain and souvenirs. Quite a novelty in Prague is the number of small private shops which are now selling pictures, jewellery and miniatures of the city's most famous sights. Most prized by visitors are the onion decor from Dubí as well as the famous Pirkenhammer china from Karlovy Vary and Brezová. Also very much in demand are paintings, small sculptures and drawings by contemporary Prague artists, which can be found in the Štvestka or U jednorožce galleries. For children, there are finely worked wooden toys – cars, trains, dolls and dolls' houses, and puppets.

Long a favourite souvenir: Bohemian glass on the Old Town Ring

ANTIQUARIAN BOOKS

There is always an opportunity to find real treasures in Prague: at the *Celetná 31* in the ★ *Antiquariat Křenek* by the Powder Tower (**109/D2**) you can chance upon old books, as well as prints and engravings. At *Karlova 2* (**108/B3**), on the other hand, they specialise in art books and old graphics. The prices are certainly pretty high.

ANTIQUES

It pays to search for some shops. Especially old clocks, Meissen porcelain or small items of furniture can be found at the following addresses: *Na příkopě 23, Karmelitská 12, Na můstku 3, Václavské náměstí 17, Maislova 17* or, 200m (650ft) from the Old Town Ring, *Kaprova Ulice 12* where one finds a shop called ★ *Antique* (**108/C2**).

BOOKS

Beautifully designed illustrated books in every language in the world are to be found in *Na příkopě 27* (**109/E2**). *Orbis* on the *Václavské náměstí 42–46* (**109/E4**) has a good contact to Bertelsmann. In Petr Vácha's shop, *Na Příkopě 3* (**109/D3**), one finds a large selection of books in various languages. A new book shop with a wide range is in the Cubist house, *Celetná 34* (**109/D2**), also rewarding is *Kafka's Bookshop at 12 Old Town Ring* (**108/C2**).

GIFTS

The entire *Karlova* (**108/B-C3**) has become a shopping arcade: there are some shops with artistically

MARCO POLO SELECTION: SHOPPING

1 Český Porcelain
One finds here, above all, high quality Bohemian porcelain produced in Dubí (page 67)

2 Christian Dior
Cosmetic consultation and facials (page 67)

3 Galerie Vlasta
Excellent lace (page 69)

4 Jungmannova
Good Supraphon brand records and CDs (page 69)

5 Kaprova ulice
Antiques on two floors (page 66)

6 Lidová jizba
Czech folk art (page 68)

7 Moser
World-famous glass wares from the former Court supplier (page 67)

8 Palace Versace
Elegant fashion house (page 68)

9 U Rotta
Fine delicatessen, wine bars in the cellar (page 68)

10 Vinohradský Pavilion
Exclusive department store and chic boutiques (page 69)

made puppets, dolls, witches and clowns that will make the hearts not only of children beat faster. Something similar will happen at *Pohádka* (fairy tales) *Celetná 32* (**109/D2**). Lovers of interior furnishings will be well served at *Art décoratif, Melantrichova 17* (**109/D3**), where one can acquire good replicas. And those wishing to decorate their apartments with faithful replicas of medieval swords, lances or armour, may even discover, at *Knight Kryštof, Kožná 8* (**108/C2**), or in the *Golden Lane 24* (**101/E4**), a chastity belt.

GLASS AND PORCELAIN

Bohemian glass and porcelain is of the world's best quality. The top wares come from the designer workshops of well-known artists. A visit to the Museum of Bohemian Glass is very rewarding (*Staroměstské náměstí 26,* **108/C2**) Among the leading producers of glass are the firms of *Moser, Crystalex, Sklo Bohemia, Kavalír* and *Rückl.* The attractive onion-decor porcelain is made in Dubí, good porcelain wares are offered by the manufacturers *Pirkenhammer, Leander* and *Thun* from Karlsbad.

Art Gallery (108/C4)
Exclusive shop with remarkable Cubist cases from the twenties. Replicas of medieval glass, Art Nouveau glass, and works of art from Blanka Adensamová are offered here. *Na Perštýně 10, Metro: Národní třída (B)*

Český Porcelain (108/C3)
★ One finds here, above all, 19th-century porcelain produced in Dubí. In those days Dubí received from Meissen the still valid license to make china. *Perlová 10, Metro: Národní třída (B)*

ERPET (108/C2)
Crystal chandeliers in all sizes and varieties. *Staroměstské náměstí 26, Metro: Staroměstská (A)*

Moser
★ The former supplier to the Imperial Court manufactures to the highest quality and design. *Na příkopě 12* (**109/D3**) *and Malé náměstí 11* (**108/C2**), *both Metro: Můstek (A)*

DEPARTMENT STORES

Bílá labut' (White Swan) (102/C5)
Na poříčí 23, Metro: Florenc (B and C)

Krone (109/E4)
Václavské náměstí 21, Metro: Můstek (A and B)

Kotva (109/E2)
Náměstí Republiky 8, Metro: Náměstí Republiky (B)

Tesco (108/C4)
Národní třída 26, Metro: Národní třída (B)

COSMETICS

Christian Dior
★ Cosmetics and facials. *Pařížská 7* (**108/C2**), *Metro: Staroměstská (A) and Národní 17* (**108/C4**), *Metro: Národní třída (B)*

Nina Ricci (108/C2)
Pařížská 4, Metro: Staroměstská (A)

ART GALLERIES

Bayer and Bayer (101/E5)
Modern art in the portal tower of the 12th-century Bishop's

Palace. *Mostecká 16, Metro: Malostranská (A)*

Pyramida **(108/B4)**
Signed glass art. *Národní 11, Metro: Národní třída (B)*

Švestka Galerie **(109/D4)**
Stars such as Andy Warhol. *Jungmannova 30, Metro: Můstek (A)*

U jednorožce **(108/D2)**
Art in Romanesque-Gothic cellars. *Staroměstské náměstí 15, Metro: Můstek (A and B)*

ARTS AND CRAFTS

A wide range of hand-woven textiles, tablecloths, puppets on a string, ceramics and articles carved in wood, at often reasonable prices, is offered by:

Lidová jizba **(109/D4)**
★ *Václavské náměstí 14, Metro: Můstek (A and B)*

Slovimex **(108/C3)**
Betlémské náměstí 2, Metro: Národní třída (B)

FOODSTUFFS AND DELICATESSEN

A gourmet will naturally also explore in Prague what is typical for this city. With various meat, fish, and cheese salads, patés and sausage varieties, the *chlebíky* (open sandwiches), will satisfy a small appetite. The wine from South Moravia is excellent. Brand-name wines, such as the red wine Roudnice, or white wine from Žernoseky must be sought in specialist wine shops. *Paris-Praha:* French patés and wines, *Jindřišská 7* (**109/E3**); *Paukert:* patés, salads, wines, *Národní třída 17* (**108/C4**); *Zlatý kříž:* open sandwiches, *Jungmannovo náměstí 19* (**109/D4**); *Dionýsos:* dozens of varieties of wine, *Vinařického 6* (**106/B3**). The ★ *U Rotta* offers in a beautiful sgraffito house with stylish wine bars, and a large selection of things to eat and drink. *Malé náměstí 3, also open Sun 1–8 pm* (**108/C2**).

FASHION

Exclusive shops are concentrated in the main thoroughfares and arcades of both the New Town and the Old Town. They are very often companies from the West, with their prices set accordingly. Nevertheless, some experts claim that their wares are cheaper in Prague. At number *3 Wenceslas Square Passage* (**109/D3**) we find the perfumery *Body Basic,* elegant shoes from *Bruno Magli,* fashion from *Daniel Hechter Paris* and the music stores in the *Bontonland Megastore.* Through the passage we then come to the street called *Na příkopě* (**109/D3–E2**): at number 4 one finds, for example, *Benetton;* one can acquire a Burberry coat from the tailor *Adam-Steiner* at number 8, *Lacoste* and *Yanni* are sold at numbers 14 and 25. Those interested in English fashion find high-quality at *Marks & Spencer* at number 19–21 as well as at the nearby *Myslbek Passage* (**109/D3**). One chooses the most beautiful ties and cravats at *The Rack,* fashion at *Marlboro Classics* and *Kookaï* or elegant shoes at *Sax.* The perfect interior furnishing design of the ★ *Palace Versace,*

Prague is still a city of art and artists

Celetná 5 (**109/D2**), complements the elegant offer of clothes, shoes and porcelain wares. Behind the six-floor shoe and leather-wares store *Bata, 6 Wenceslas Square* (**109/D3**), one can buy something chic in the store of *Hugo Boss, Jungmannovo náměstí* (**109/D4**). There is a great number of shops and boutiques in ★ *Pavillon, Vinohradská 50* (**108/D2**), which also offer a colorful range of goods.

NUMISMATICS

Old medals and coins for collectors are to be found at *Pařížská 8* (**108/C2**).

RECORDS

Jazz, pop and classics on vinyl records or CDs are good quality and always sold at reasonable prices. Classical music can also be found at the excellent old store ★ *Supraphon, Jungmannova 20* (**109/D4**). There is a large selection of jazz and pop music to be found at *Popron, Jungmannova 30* (**109/D4**). A super-store is the *Bontonland Megastore, Václavské náměstí 1 in the Passage* (**109/D3**).

JEWELLERY

When buying jewellery one should give particular attention to the authenticity of the hallmark. However, there is no problem with jewellery featuring Bohemian garnets. The choice is also enormous for silver, goldplating and stones set in 14 carat gold. One can buy at reasonable prices at *Granát, Dlouhá třída 28* (**109/D1**). Replicas of old jewellery in silver 900/000 are also offered there. One pays much more along the Royal Route, where *Český Granát* has three branches: *Celetná 4* (**109/D2**); *Karlova 44* (**108/C3**); and *Mostecká 3* (**101/E5**). Fully qualified goldsmiths are to be found at *Na příkopě: Halada* number 16 and *Dušák* number 17 (**109/D3**).

LACE

Belgium's Queen Fabiola presented the modern work of Vlasta Wasserbauerová at the 1988 Exhibion of Lace.

Galerie Vlasta (**108/C2**)
★ *Staroměstské náměstí 5, Metro: Staroměstská (A)*

A good night's sleep

New top hotels and charming little luxury hotels, bed and breakfast at sensible prices. One can spend a comfortable night at a reasonable price in private rooms and pensions

In Prague one could always find good accommodation, even during the time of communism. To accommodate the steady flow of tourists a number of new, luxury hotels have recently been built, while some of the traditional establishments have been completely modernized, and many of the larger hotels have increased their capacity.

Several of the grand old residences, once homes to the nobility, have been renovated and converted into small, luxury hotels. With just a dozen or so rooms, the atmosphere is intimate and they offer the comfort and charm of a bygone age. Hotels are divided into the normal categories: 5-star luxury, 5-star, 4-star, and so forth. The top hotels, such as the Hotel InterContinental and the Diplomat, offer everything you would expect: 24-hour room service, colour TVs and hotel teletext, business centres and conference rooms etc. The largest four-star hotel, the Prague Hilton Atrium, has 1568 rooms. Room prices are in line with

The Evropa, opened in 1900, is a monument to the glory of Art Nouveau

those charged by equivalent hotels in other major European cities, but they are slightly lower out of season.

It is usual to book half-board at a hotel. The food in a good number of the hotel restaurants is first-class, with menus offering fine Bohemian and international dishes. Although many hotels offer half-board, you may prefer to try out the small, atmospheric eateries dotted around the Little Quarter and Staré Me sto.

Bed and breakfast hotels are another recent development. Although generally located outside the town centre, they offer tourists a high standard of accommodation at very reasonable prices. Bear in mind, however, that toilets and bathrooms are shared, usually one per two double rooms. An even cheaper option are the small guest houses on the edge of town and the privately owned houses which rent rooms that have generally been refurbished. The special enchantment of private accommodation is the immediate contact with one's host.

Reasonably priced student houses are not only available to the young – generally during the half-term holidays. They are further away from the city center, but the well organized Prague public transport system brings guests quickly into the heart of the city.

The people of Prague like to eat well – and copiously! Breakfast in hotels or private rooms tends to be quite ample. Breakfasts at hotels or private rooms can be more substantial than in Paris. Breakfast is included at most accommodation. Some hotels also offer a Scandinavian-style breakfast to guests residing elsewhere. At an all-inclusive price one can have hot and cold food, and drinks, at a breakfast buffet.

Those wishing to book accommodation by telephone or fax from home, must first dial the international code 004202, followed by the hotel's number. The *Pragotur Agency* assists in booking private accommodation and hotels in all categories: Za Poříčskou branou 7 (**103/D5**), Tel: 24 81 61 20, Fax: 24 81 61 72, Metro: Florenc (B and C). The *Key System* agency books overnight stays in 1,500 rooms of all the categories. Tel: 21 00 15 40, Fax: 21 00 15 44, E-mail address: keypr@mailserv.bohem-net.cz.

CATEGORY 1 HOTELS

For those demanding luxury, from 3600 Kč per double room

Ambassador (109/D3)
★ Art Nouveau building on Wenceslas Square. Most of the rooms are in the Louis XIV style. French restaurant, game dishes in the Halali Grill. 'Goldfingers' strip show. *174 rooms, Václavské náměstí 5, Tel: 24 19 31 11,* *Fax: 24 23 06 20, Metro: Můstek (A and B)*

Esplanade (109/E4)
★ Exxclusive hotel in the Art Déco style in a quiet location close to Wenceslas Square. French restaurant with international cuisine, 'Est Wine Restaurant', and live music. *64 rooms. Washingtonova 19, Tel: 24 21 17 15, Fax: 24 22 93 06, Metro: Muzeum (A and C)*

Holiday Inn (101/D2)
Built in the wedding-cake style of the 1950s, but fully modernized, this hotel is some distance outside the city. Good Bohemian and international cuisine, and a wine bar with folk music. *251 rooms, 2 for the handicapped; Dejvice, Koulova 15, Tel: 24 39 31 11, Fax: 24 31 06 16, Metro: Dejvická (A)*

Mövenpick Hotel Prague (105/D3)
★ Convenient location only 4km from the end of the Pilsen motorway. Two hotel buildings on different levels, connected by a cable car. The German chef of the excellent Il Giardino luxury restaurant surprises with exclusive fish dishes. Underground parking. *435 comfortable rooms, 4 for the handicapped, Mozartova 1, Tel: 57 15 11 11, Fax: 57 15 31 31, Metro: Anděl (B), then a 300m walk*

Panorama (O)
A 24-storey hotel not too far from the Prague-Brno motorway, opposite the Hotel Forum in Pankrác. Good for long-distance travellers. The hotel has a sauna, pool and solarium. *451 rooms and 2 apartments, Prag 4, Milevská 7, Tel: 61 16 11 11, Fax: 42 62 25, Metro: Pankrác (C)*

MARCO POLO SELECTION: HOTELS

1 Ambassador
Venerable hotel on
Wenceslas Square (page 72)

2 Esplanade
Good location opposite
a park (page 72)

3 Evropa
Classic example of the Art
Nouveau style (page 75)

4 Kampa
Quiet hotel on Kampa Island
with all modern comforts
(page 75)

5 Mövenpick Hotel Prague
Main building and annexe
connected by a cable car
(page 72)

6 Prague Hilton Atrium
The largest hotel in Prague,
788 rooms, 2 tennis courts
(page 74)

7 Renaissance
High-tech hotel, centrally
located (page 73)

8 U Blaženky
In quiet villa area close to
the end of the Pilsen-Prague
motorway (page 76)

9 Vaníček
Terrace hotel in a quiet
location (page 73)

10 White House
A small and fine place to
stay (page 77)

Paříž   (109/E2)

Built in 1907, this hotel boasts
very large rooms. The restaurant,
Sarah Bernhard, with its Italian
mosaic decoration, serves Bohemian and international cuisine in
a pleasant fin-de-siècle atmosphere. With a lovely Art Nouveau
café. *100 rooms. U obecního domu 1,
Tel: 24 22 21 51, Fax: 24 22 54 75,
Metro: Náměstí Republiky (B)*

Parkhotel   (102/C3)

Elegant hotel by Stromovka Park
in Letná. Modern restaurant with
Bohemian cuisine, bar-grill and
wine bar with good food. Casino
open from 8 pm to 5 am. Parking. *324 rooms. Veletržní 20, Tel: 20
13 11 11, Fax: 24 31 61 80, Metro:
Vltavská (C)*

Renaissance   (109/E2)

★ A new and well-appointed
hotel, not far from the Powder
Tower. *309 rooms, V celnici 7, Tel:
24 81 03 96, Fax: 23 81 16 87, Metro: Náměstí Republiky (B)*

Vaníček (T)   (100/C6)

★ ⚐ Guests at this family-run
luxury establishment enjoy an
unrivalled panorama of Prague.
The hotel includes a good, reasonably priced restaurant with
excellent service. Nice terraces
with barbecue. Double room
2700 Kč in winter, 3800 Kč during the summer season. Shuttle
buses serve central Prague.
There is a 7 percent reduction
when you pay cash. *18 rooms, Na
Hřebenkách 60, Tel: 35 07 14, Fax:
35 06 19, Metro: Karlovo náměstí
(B) and bus 176*

CATEGORY 2 HOTELS

*Medium-priced hotels from under
3600 Kč per double room*

Prague Luxury Hotels

Adria   (109/D4)
This 4-star hotel in the center of the city has been totally renovated. Good international and Bohemian cooking in the Restaurant Triton. *67 rooms, 1 for the handicapped, from 4000 Kč, Václavské náměstí 26, Tel: 24 21 65 43, Fax: 24 21 10 25, Metro: Můstek (A and B)*

Diplomat   (101/D3)
Towards the airport. An exclusive, technically refined hotel. Conference rooms for 8 to 350 people. Underground car park. *382 rooms, from 7200 Kč, Dejvice, Evropská třída 15, Tel: 24 39 41 11, Fax: 2 39 42 15, Metro: Dejvická (A)*

Forum   (106/C4)
Near the motorway to Brno. Bowling, squash. *531 rooms, 5 for the handicapped, from 7200 Kč, Nusle, Kongresová, Tel: 61 19 12 18, Fax: 42 06 84, Metro: Vyšehrad (C)*

Hoffmeister   (101/F5)
Luxury hotel in post-modern flamboyant style, Very comfortable, fully air-conditioned. Restaurant Ada and Lily wine bar. Excellent food. Underground parking. *44 rooms, from 6300 Kč, Pod Bruskou 9, Tel: 57 31 09 42, Fax: 53 09 59, Metro: Malostranská (A)*

InterContinental   (102/B5)
Quiet location on the banks of the Vltava, lovely panoramic view of city from upper floors of this 5-star house. Underground parking. *365 rooms, 1 for the handicapped, from 8600 Kč, Náměstí Curieových 5, Tel: 24 88 11 11, Fax: 24 81 11 98, Metro: Staroměstská (A)*

Palace   (109/E3)
This beautiful Art Nouveau building (1906), is a 5-star house, fully renovated in 1989. Opposite the main post office, a stone's throw from Wenceslas Square. Casino, sauna, solarium, underground parking. *125 rooms, from 7200, 7800, or 9000 Kč according to season, Panská 12, Tel: 24 09 31 11, Fax: 24 22 12 40, Metro: Můstek (A and B)*

Prague Hilton Atrium   (103/D4)
★ Modern hotel built by a French company in the centre of the city. Largest hotel in Prague with business service centre, conference rooms and restaurants. *788 rooms, from 6650 Kč, Pobřežní ulice, Tel: 24 84 11 11, Fax: 24 81 18 96, Metro: Florenc (B and C)*

Savoy   (100/C5)
Excellent five-star Art Nouveau hotel near Prague Castle. Fully modernised, exclusive Restaurat Hradčany, live piano music. Jazz brunch every Sunday 11 am–2 pm. French, Mexican, and Italian dishes. *58 rooms, from 7600 Kč, Keplerova 6, Tel: 243 02 11, Fax: 24 30 21 28, Metro: Hradčanská (A)*

Admirál Botel   **(105/F3)**
This botel consists of four boats moored on the banks of the Vltava and converted into hotels, not far from the Plzenská (the Pilsen motorway). *88 twin-bed cabins, shower, WC, 1700–2400 Kč, Hořejší nábřeží, Tel: 57 32 13 02, Fax: 54 96 16, Metro: Anděl (B)*

Albatros Botel   **(102/C4)**
◁▷ This boat-hotel is anchored close to the center of town with a lovely view of the Hradschin. *86 rooms, 1700–2200 Kč, Nábřeží Ludvíka Svobody, Tel: 24 81 05 47, Fax: 24 81 12 14, Metro: Náměstí Republiky (B), then an 800m walk*

Belvedere   **(102/C3)**
A nice hotel in a pleasant area of Prague (Letná). It features a restaurant, a snack bar, and a brass band on Thursdays. *117 rooms, 1650–3600 Kč, Milady Horákové 19, Tel: 37 47 41, Fax: 33 37 23 68, Metro: Vltavská (B)*

Coubertin   **(104/C2)**
A modern house with restaurant in a quiet part of Strahov. *25 rooms, 1600–2400 Kč, Atletická 4, Tel: 35 28 51, Fax: 20 51 32 08, Metro: Karlovo náměstí (B) and Bus 176*

Dientzenhofer   **(101/E6)**
At the birthplace of the 16th-century Prague Baroque master Kilian Ignaz Dientzenhofer, guests are surround by the Baroque and all manner of comfort. Parking in the courtyard. *6 rooms for the handicapped, 2500 Kč, Nosticova 2, Tel and Fax: 24 51 11 93, Metro: Malostranská (A)*

Evropa   **(109/E4)**
★ A classic example of Prague Art Nouveau architecture with many beautiful interior details in the café and Pilsner Restaurant. *104 rooms, 2250–3500 Kč, Václavské náměstí 29, Tel and Fax: 24 22 81 17, Metro: Muzeum (A)*

Golf   **(O)**
The hotel is near a golf course and just 2 km (1.3 mi) from the Pilsen-Prague motorway. *174 rooms, 2000–2700 Kč, Plzeňská 215 a, Tel: 52 32 51, Fax: 57 21 52 13, Metro: Anděl (B), trams 4 and 9*

Junior   **(105/B2)**
Located in the city center on a very lively street. All rooms are equipped with a shower and a WC. Restaurant. *22 rooms, 2000 Kč, Žitná 12, Tel: 29 29 84, Fax: 24 22 39 11, Metro: Muzeum (A) or Karlovo náměstí (B)*

Kampa   **(105/E1)**
★ This completely modernised Little Quarter house, known as *The Old Armoury*, is located in a tranquil spot on Kampa Island. Restaurant (7 am–10 pm). *84 rooms, 2500–3200 Kč, Všehrdova 16, Tel: 57 32 08 37, Fax: 57 32 02 62, Metro: Národní třída (B), tram 9, second stop: Újezd*

Karl Inn   **(103/F4)**
This new three-star hotel is not far from the city center. *168 rooms, 1750–2600 Kč, Šaldova 54, Tel: 24 81 17 18, Fax: 24 81 26 81, Metro: Křižíkova (B)*

Kern   **(104/B4)**
A quiet, family-oriented atmosphere prevails in this popular establishment. Located in an exclusive residential area west of the city, about 4km (3 mi) from the end of the Pilsen motorway. Parking in the courtyard. *14 rooms,*

Pyramida (100/C6)

This hotel, which has been constructed in the shape of a pyramid, is located not far from Prague Castle. *350 rooms, 2500–3000 Kč, Břevnov, Bělohorská 24, Tel:. 311 32 41, Fax: 35 00 30, Metro: Hradčanská (A), tram 8*

Racek Botel (O)

In the southern part of the city, somewhere between Vyšehrad and Braník, one finds the third of the unusual and fascinating Prague boat-hotels at its mooring. It also has a bar with live music. *86 rooms, 1800–2500 Kč, Na Dvoreckého louce, Tel: 61 21 41 09, Fax: 61 21 43 83, Metro: Karlovo náměstí (B)*

U Blaženky (At Blaženka) (104/D3)

★ This is a small, quite comfortable hotel located in a quiet residential area about 5km (3mi) from the end of the Pilsen motorway. *9 rooms and 4 apartments, 2300– 26 2900 Kč, U Blaženky 1, Tel and Fax: 24 51 10 29, Metro: Anděl (B), bus 137, third stop*

Hotel Forum: international-style hotel on the outskirts of Prague

2000 Kč, Jinonická 50, Tel and Fax: 57 21 08 76, Metro: Anděl (B), trams 4 and 9, bus 130

The Flemish Spy

The next time you reach for your wallet in Prague, take a closer look at the Czech banknotes, which were designed by Karel Kulhánek. During the Communist regime, the artist was arrested and charged with trying to make the country appear ridiculous in the eyes of the outside world – an accusation for which Kulhánek was incarcerated. His wife wrote to him in prison, informing him that the police had confiscated his passport, and therefore he would no longer be able to go and visit his old friend Hieronymous Bosch. When a representative from the Czech secret police intercepted the letter, he was incensed and roared at Kulhánek: 'Who does this Bosch work for? What secret information have you passed along to him?' While attempting to keep a straight face, Kulhánek respectfully replied that the artist had been dead for 500 years. In reply to this, the policeman grumbled, 'bloody intellectuals'.

CATEGORY 3 HOTELS

From 900–1800 Kč (double)

Balkán (105/F3)
Basic hotel in the Smíchov quarter of the city on a very busy road. The rooms facing the courtyard are quieter. *28 rooms with shower and WC, 1400 Kč, Tel: 54 07 77, Fax: 54 06 70, Ulice Svornosti 28, Metro: Anděl (B), then a 300m walk*

Kolej Komenského (100/C5)
A former student residence, occasionally used as a bed and breakfast hotel. Not far from the Castle. Rooms available in July and August. *150 rooms, 750 Kč, Parléřova 6, Tel: 352 04 15, Metro: Hradčanská (A)*

Kupa (O)
This bed and breakfast hotel is located in the south of Prague at the last stop on the Metro line C. *560 rooms, from 1250 Kč, between Háje and Chodov, Kupeckého 843, Tel: 791 03 21, Fax: 791 02 16, Metro: Háje (C), then a short two minutes' walk.*

White House (104/A6)
★ The pension lies conveniently on the west side of the city, around 4km (3 mi) from the end of the Pilsen motorway. Very quiet. Parking area. Small swimming pool. *13 rooms and 3 apartments, 1600 Kč, Markova 10, Tel: 57 21 33 17, Metro: Jinonice (B), then a 300m walk*

FOR YOUNG PEOPLE

Student houses
Universitas Tour arranges reasonably priced accommodation: *Opletalova 38, Tel: 26 04 26, Fax: 24 21 22 90, Metro: Hlavní nádraží (C).* A second agency is *Koleje a menzy univerzity Karlovy* (Charles University student union): *Voršilská 1, Tel: 29 26 24, Fax: 29 00 73, Metro: Národní třída (B)*

Hostel Estec (100/C6)
This student house on the Strahov hill is converted into reasonably priced accommodation from July to August. *550 beds, Vaníčkova 5, Tel: 52 73 44, Metro: Dejvická (A), buses 217 and 143 or Metro: Karlovo náměstí (B), bus 176, Stadion Strahov stop*

Hostel Sokol (105/E1)
The house lies in the Little Quarter (Malá Strana) and is open only from May to September. Reasonable price with own sleeping bag and sheets. *Hellichova 1, Tel: 24 51 06 07, Metro: Národní třída (B), tram 22*

Kolej Jednota (109/F2)
The house is in the heart of Prague and only a few minutes from the main railway station (Hlavní nádraží). *Opletalova 38, Tel: 26 04 26, Metro: Hlavní nádraží (C)*

Travelers' Hostels (109/D1)
Seven student houses with 900 beds. Overnight stay with breakfast from from 200–400 Kč. *Central office, Dlouhá 33, Tel: 231 13 18, Fax: 231 61 61, Metro: Národní třída (B)*

Větrník (100/A5)
Student house. 1000 beds from July to August, 40 outside the holiday period. *Na větrníku 12, Tel: 29 00 73, Fax: 29 26 24, Metro: Hradčanská (A), buses 1 and 18*

Prague diary

As in all famous cities, there is no shortage of top-class entertainment in Prague, from folk-dancing, classical concerts, to jazz and pop music

The people of Prague excel in the art of entertainment. After so many years of cultural repression, the streets of the city are animated once again. The annual festivities begin on New Year' Eve which is celebrated on Wenceslas Square ★. The arrival of spring in Prague brings with it a wonderful, colourful atmosphere. Snowdrops and violets are sold on street corners and, at Easter, farmers' wives from South Moravia – often dressed in traditional costume – come into the city to sell their intricately hand-painted Easter eggs. On May 1, young people lay bouquets of flowers at the memorial to the writer K. H. Mácha on Petřín. From the middle of May to the beginning of June, Prague resonates with music – the 'Prague Spring' festival traditionally opens with a rousing rendition of Smetana's *My Country* by the Prague Philharmonic, and closes with Beethoven's *Ninth Symphony*. In addition to these festiv-

In the garden of the Bertramka Summer Residence, in which Mozart was often a guest, his works, above all, are played during the 'Prague Spring' music festival

ities, a great number of concerts are staged in the intervening weeks, and folk groups perform southern Bohemian polkas and stirring Moravian folk songs in Prague's gardens and halls throughout the summer months. Concerts are held daily in the city's grandest venues, the Rudolfinum, in the Bertramka, the 'House at the Stone Bell', the Spanish Hall, in the Smetana Hall at the Klementinum, the gardens of the Old Palace, and the surrounding churches. Perhaps the most beautiful of all these concert venues is the salon in the Nostic Palace. Many jazz and rock concerts are also staged here, including some big names, drawing in a young and lively crowd. In the autumn are the opening performances held at Prague's ballet, theatre and three opera houses, and by the creative *Laterna Magika* company. On 28 October, a major music festival is held to celebrate the anniversary of the birth of the Czech Republic, with everything from wind ensembles to hard rock played by groups that gather in the city's public squares. A party spirit prevails across the country on 17 November, the anniversary of the Velvet Revolution. At Christmas time, many churches erect nativity scenes. A beautiful Baroque scene (1764) with figures that are almost life-size, can be seen at St Mary's Church in the Capucin monastery, not far from Loreta.

NATIONAL HOLIDAYS

1 January; Easter Monday; 1 May; 8 May; 5 July (*Introduction of Christianity*); 6 July (*Death of Jan Hus*); 28 October (*Founding of the Czech Republic, 1918*); 24 to 26 December. Museums and restaurants remain open on public holidays, while shops and businesses are closed.

SPECIAL EVENTS

January

Beginning of January: *Prague Winter* – an important week of cultural festivities. A variety of events and performances in theatres, churches, and concert halls.

January 5th: *The Three Holy Kings* ride in a spectacular parade on their camels from Hradčanský in Loreto Square.

February

Numerous balls at the hotels Diplomat, Forum, Prague Hilton Atrium and in the Palace of Culture.

March

Almost throughout the month: *Festival of Contemporary Music*

April

Beginning of April: *International Jazz Festival* held in the Music Bar Lucerna

May

★ Mid-May to early June: *Prague Spring*. Music festival with many different orchestras and soloists from abroad. The festival opens with Smetana's *My Fatherland*, and finishes with Beethoven's *Ninth Symphony* at the Rudolfinum.

May to October: *Festival of Jewish Culture* in the Great Synagogue in the Jeruzalémská

MARCO POLO SELECTION: EVENTS

1 The Royal Bohemian Crown Insignia
They are seldom exhibited (page 81)

2 Prague Spring Festival
The city is full of music (page 80)

3 Prague Autumn
Music festival with Prague orchestras and the like from abroad (page 81)

4 New Year's Eve
Celebrated everywhere (page 79)

5 Dance Prague
The Prague Orchestra accompanying a variety of international soloists (page 81)

6 Nativity Cribs
They enhance almost all of the churches (page 81)

Folk dancing and rural traditions are still very much alive

June

Mid-June to early July: ★ *Dance Prague.* International Festival of Contemporary Dance (various venues and Old Town Ring).

Final weekend: *International Folklore Festival* in Strážnice

July

July to the middle of September: *Prague Folklore Festival* in the City Library. Folklore groups from Bohemia, Moravia, and Slovakia.

Third weekend: *International Agharta Jazz Festival* in the Music Bar Lucerna

August

Mid-August: three-week *Verdi Festival* at the State Opera House.

Final weekend: *Grand Prix* motorcycle racing in Brno

September

Second weekend: *PRAGA International Exhibition of Philately* at the Post Museum.

★ Second and third weeks in September: Music festival *Prague Autumn* in the Dvořák Hall the Rudolfinum

Second half of September: *Festival of the German Language Theatre* in Prague. German, Austrian, Swiss, as well as Czech and Slovak ensembles perform.

Late September to early November: *Festival Musica Sacra Praga* in the Betlémská Chapel

October

Second week in October: *International Glass Trade Fair.*

★ October 28th: *Day of the founding of the Czechoslovakian Republic in 1918.* On this occasion, the Royal Bohemian Crown Insignia will be exhibited for the entire week.

November

November 17th: *Anniversary of the Velvet Revolution of 1989*

December

★ Carved nativity cribs are exhibited in the churches from Christmas Eve to early February. Worth seeing: St Vitus Cathedral and the Church of the Assumption at the Capucin Monastery on Loretánské náměstí.

Out on the town

*Opera and pantomime, classical concerts and jazz,
musicals and discos, traditional bands in old pubs –
Prague's nightlife is richly varied*

Prague specializes in musical and comic entertainment. The famous *Laterna Magica* always has something amusing and many surprises. At the cabaret *U Fleků* the mood intensifies with every glass of beer, and cameo scenes in which the humour knows no bounds, are as profuse as the stars in the sky. The old tradition of music is not only alive in the concert halls, but also in the streets and the pubs in which brass bands abound.

BOAT TRIPS

An experience for young and old are the excursion trips on the Vltava, for example, on the two almost 60-year-old paddle steamers V*ltava* and *Vyšehrad* in the evening, with a meal on board in the restaurant with musical entertainment. Short and long panorama trips through Prague are offered to the end of the Slapy Valley and to the zoo. Bookings: *Čedok, Na příkopě 18,*

*The Prague National Theatre
has its classics: Smetana operas
are performed regularly*

Metro: Můstek (A and B) (**109/D3**); *Paroplavba, Rašínovo nábřeží, on the Palackého Bridge, Metro: Karlovo náměstí (B)* (**105/A3**); *EDP, Na Františku, by the Hotel InterContinental, Metro: Staroměstská (A)* (**102/B4**)

DISCOTHEQUES

Rap, hard-rock, ethno – everything that's fashionable comes to Prague.

Lávka Club (108/B3)
⚊ Top address for not only young people. Also dancing on the terrace in the garden. *Daily 9 pm– 5 am; 1 Novotného lávka, by the Smetana Museum, Metro: Staro městská (A)*

Modrá terasa (109/D3)
Oldies disco, music from the sixties to the nineties. Variety programme every Friday and Saturday. *Daily 10 pm–5 am; Na příkopě 1, Metro: Můstek (A and B)*

Musicpark (107/D2)
The largest disco in the city, also café, restaurant, pub, and casino. *Daily except Mon, 9 pm–5 am; Francouzská 4, Tel: 691 14 91, Metro: Náměstí míru (A)*

International musicians were playing good jazz in Prague before the war when one liked to shake a leg to the foxtrot. Jazz in Prague today is played at a very high level because the musicians are the cream of performers: the flute virtuoso Jiří Stivín, pianist Emil Viklický, Peter Lípa, The Original Synkopický Orchestra, conducted by O. Havelka, or the Petr Binder Blues Band. The best jazz music is played in the ★ *Reduta*, a club founded in 1958 and thus the oldest club still operating in Europe. The president of the USA, Bill Clinton, appeared there in January of 1994 with his saxophone versions of *My Funny Valentine* and *Summertime*. Václav Havel accompanied him, shrugging off rhythmic error with his spontaneous charm. *Reduta, Národní třída 20* (**108/C4**); *Agharta Jazz Centre (with Jazz Shop and Jazz Café), Krakovská 5* (**109/E5**); *Metropolitan Jazz Club, Jungmannova 14* (**109/D4**); *U malého Glena, reggae and acid jazz, Karmelitská 12* (**101/E5**); *U staré paní, Michalská 9* (**108/C3**); *Music Bar Lucerna, Vodičkova 36* (**109/D4**)

CABARET AND REVUES

The Prague cabaret and revue scene offers entertainment for all tastes: the range is from American strip shows to Old Prague cabaret and folklore cimbalom music. Some stages offer Black Theatre – actors clothed in black move with objects against a black background, and behind the light screen the objects appear to be floating through the air.

Goldfingers (109/D3)

★ This exclusive American strip show at the Alhambra offers much beauty and sensuality, albeit with a lack of imagination. *Daily from 9 pm, Tel: 24 19 38 56, Václavské náměstí 5, Metro: Můstek (A and B)*

Holiday Inn Hotel (101/D1)

★ Wine parties with cimbalom music and fiery folk songs take place here in the garden pavilion. *Daily 7.30 pm; Dejvice, Koulova 15, Tel: 24 39 31 11, Metro: Dejvická (A), buses 107, 147, 160, 1st stop*

Reduta Theater (108/C4)

The extremely humorous performance *Anatomy of a Kiss* belongs to the sphere of the Prague Black Theatre. *Národní třída 20, Tel: 24 23 70 74, Metro: Národní třída (B)*

U Fleků (108/C5)

★ ☻ The epitome of Old Bohemian cabaret: with a beer with 13% original wort, old worldwide hits and couplets are sung and danced to with temperament. *Tues–Sat from 7 pm; Křemencova 11, Tel: 24 91 51 18, Metro: Národní třída (B)*

Varieté Praga (109/D4)

A traditional establishment with an international programme, artists and a dance show. *Vodičkova 30, Tel: 24 21 59 45, music and dancing Tues–Sun from 7.30 pm, programme from 9.30 pm, Metro: Můstek (A and B)*

COMMERCIAL SEX

Until recently Prague was a decent city. But that was not in accord with the temperament of

MARCO POLO SELECTION: ENTERTAINMENT

1 Alhambra
'Goldfingers' strip show
(page 84)

2 Laterna Magika
Known throughout the
world (page 87)

3 Křižík Fountain
Music, aquatic choreo-
graphy and coloured
lighting (page 85)

4 Puppet Theatre
Don Giovanni sings here as
a puppet in his best Italian
(page 88)

5 Musical Krysař
The *Pied Piper* in Theatera
Ta Fantastica (page 86)

**6 Národní divadlo
(National Theatre)**
Opera and ballet events
are held in the Golden
Chapel (page 86)

7 Radost FX
The best night club in
Prague (page 86)

8 Reduta Jazz
Traditional jazz (page 84)

9 U Fleků
Old Bohemian cabaret with
a fine beer (page 84)

10 Wine parties
Cimbalom music with
folk songs and dancing
(page 84)

the people who enjoyed a certain freedom of morals, as we know from the literature of Milan Kundera or Pavel Kohout. At this time the Town Hall is attempting to force out the ladies from the Perlová.

CONCERTS

Prague is a wonderful place for classical music lovers. The Czech Philharmonic, the Prague Symphony Orchestra FOK and the Prague Radio Symphony Orchestra perform all year round. Numerous concerts are performed by the Prague Mozart Orchestra, playing in original 18th-century costumes, the Musica Bohemica, Czech Nonettes and the Smetana Quartet are held in such splendid venues as the Mirrored Chapel of the Klementinum, the 'House at the Stone Bell', in Liechtenstein Palace, the Spanish Hall, the Dvořák Museum, and the Mozart Museum at Bertramka. During the summer season, concerts are also held in the beautifully landscaped Prague Palace Gardens. Glorious church music can be heard in St Vitus Cathedral, and in the churches of St Nicholas and St Jakob. Programme guides are produced monthly.

SON ET LUMIERE

The ★ Křižík Fountain (**102/C2**), located at the old Trade Fair Hall offers onlookers an evening of unforgettable artistic experience in a multimedia style, comprising music, aquatic choreography, and colourful lighting effects. *Výstaviště, Metro: Holešovické nádraží (C), trams 5, 12 and 17*

MUSICALS

A new musicals scene has formed in Prague. Well produced performances of foreign and Czech musicals take place at: *Výstaviště Theatre Spirála*: *Jesus Christ Superstar*; *Theatre Pyramida*: *Vlasy (Hair)*; ★ *Theatre Ta Fantastica*: *Krysař (Pied Piper)*; *Hudební divadlo v Karlíně (music theatre in Karlín)*: *Hello, Dolly!*

NIGHT CLUBS

Radost FX   (106/C3)
★ The best night club in Prague and a complex of lounges with live music, disco, café and restaurant. Brunch every weekend in American style: *11 am–3pm; Bělehradská 120, Tel: 24 25 47 76, Metro: Náměstí Míru (A)*

Roxy   (109/D1)
Rock concerts, techno parties, dance music. *Daily 9 pm–5 am; Dlouhá 33, Tel: 24 81 76 86, Metro: Náměstí Republiky (B)*

OPERA AND BALLET

On the Smetana Quay stands the beautiful Neo-Renaissance Národní divadlo (National Theatre), fondly known as the 'Golden Chapel on the Vltava' among the people of Prague. The classic show here is Smetana's opera *Libuše*. Not far from the National Museum is the Prague State Opera (Státní opera Praha), the former New German Theatre, with its lovely neo-Rococo interior. Mozart's *Don Giovanni* premiered at the Stavovské divadlo (now the shiny green and gold Estates Theatre), near the centre of the city, in 1787. All three theatres stage world class opera and ballet performances, except during the summer months.

Národní divadlo
(National Theatre)   (108/B4)
★ Not only for Smetana fans. *Národní třída 2, Tel: 24 91 42 04, Metro: Národní třída (B)*

Opera Galas   (109/D2)
Famous arias and duets – among the soloists are Russians and Italians – in the Gothic ambiance of the 'House at the Stone Bell'. *Staroměstské náměstí 13, Tel: 24 22 43 51, Metro: Staroměstská (A)*

Státní opera Praha
(Prague State Opera)   (109/F4)
Operas in their original languages with English subtitles above the stage. *Wilsonova 4, Tel:*

Coq au vin instead of dumplings

A brand new phenomenon of the Prague gastronomic scene: it ia becoming increasingly international. Many new establishments are run by foreigners, and from the ambiance to the head waiter, all is from outside of Bohemia. In *Fakhreldine* are twelve Arabian cooks, a cuisinier from Dijon creates magic at *La Provence*, there are German cooks at *Mövenpick* and in *Penta*. In *Red Hot And Blues*, *Little Glen*, *Oscar's* and in *Jo's Bar*, one speaks American English, the *James Joyce* brought Irish flair to Prague. A touch of the California way of life in central Europe: *The Globe* – a café run by Scott Rogers from San Francisco.

The people of Prague are enthusiastic fans of the cinema

24 22 76 93 and 24 22 98 98, Metro: Muzeum (A and C)

Stavovské divadlo
(Guild Theatre) (109/D3)
The works performed here are
synchronized in English. *Ovocný
trh 1, Tel: 24 21 50 01 and 24 22
85 03, Metro: Můstek (A and B)*

Almost every visitor to Prague
wishes to see at least once the
good old *Laterna Magika*, which
was presented for the first time
with great success in 1958 in
Brussels. There have been more
than 4500 performances since
then. The Puppet Theatre, with
its over 800 performances of
Don Giovanni, and the Black
Theater both have a magical attraction for the public.

Laterna Magika (108/B4)
★ In this Czech invention,
which was received enthusiasti-
cally at the 1958 Expo World Exhibition, a film or slide projection
is combined with stage performances. *Theatre Nová scéna,
Národní 4 (next to the National
Theatre), Tel: 24 91 41 29, Fax: 24
22 75 67, Metro: Národní třída (B)*

Puppet Theater (108/C2)

★ One of the hits of the Prague theatre season is Mozart's *Don Giovanni*: *Žatecká 1, Tel: 232 34 29, Metro: Náměstí Republiky (B)*

Black Theatre Image (108/C2)

The wonder of the Black Theater and pantomime. *Daily 8 pm; closed December 1–24 and all through January, Pařížská 4, Tel: 232 91 91, Metro: Staroměstská (A)*

ROCK MUSIC

The Prague rock clubs are of a high level. Recommended: *Belmondo Revival Club, Sept–June, Bubenská 1, Metro: Vltavská (C)* **(103/D3)**; *Bunkr (with café), Lodecká 2, Metro: Náměstí Republiky (B)* **(109/F1)**; *Rock Café, Národní třída 20, Metro: Národní třída (B)* **(108/C4)**; *Rock Club Újezd, Újezd 18, Metro: Národní třída (B)* **(101/E6)**; *Legenda, Křižovnická 12, Metro: Staroměstská (A)* **(108/B2)**

CASINOS

Admirál (109/D4)

American roulette, poker, black jack. *Daily 1 pm–5 am; Vodičkova 30, Metro: Můstek (A and B)*

Casino Blue Diamond (103/D4)

Gambling at the Hotel Prague Hilton Atrium. *Daily 2 pm–6 am; Pobřežní 1, Metro: Florenc (B and C)*

Casino Palais Savarin (109/D3)

American roulette, black jack and poker. *Daily 1 pm–4 am; Na příkopě 10, Metro: Můstek (A and B)*

Forum Hotel (106/C4)

Three tables with American roulette, two with black jack. *Daily 8 pm–4 am; Nusle, Kongresová 1, Metro: Vyšehrad (C)*

Parkhotel (102/C3)

Casino with American roulette and black jack. *Daily 8 pm–5 am; Veletržní 20, Metro: Vltavská (C)*

WINE BARS WITH LIVE ROMANY MUSIC

Halali Restaurant (109/D3)

Game specialities and Hungarian cuisine at the Hotel Ambassador. *Daily 6 pm–3 am; Václavské náměstí 5–7, Tel: 24 19 36 89, Metro: Můstek (A and B)*

Šumická vinárna (108/C4)

❖ With a good meal in the deep cellars one drinks a lovely dry Pavlovice wine from the cask. The fiery Romany band will accompany you with such passionate melodies that one is liable to gravitate to the dance floor after an excellent meal. *Sun–Fri 12 am–3 pm and 6–12 pm, Sat 6–12 pm; Mikulandská 12 (corner of Národní třída), Tel: 24 91 21 30, Metro: Národní třída (B)*

Useful Words and Phrases

Yes	Ano	How much?	Kolik?
No	Ne	Good evening	Dobrý večer
Hello	ahoj	Excuse me	Prosím
Good day	Dobrý den	Sorry	Promiňte
Goodbye	Na shledanou	Do you speak	Mluvíte anglicky?
Thank-you	Děkuji	English?	

Castle, Charles Bridge and More

These walking tours are marked in green on the outside back flap and in the street atlas beginning on page 100

① ART NOUVEAU BUILDINGS ALONG THE VLTAVA

 Other than Brussels, no other European city has so many Art Nouveau buildings as Prague. A three-hour walk.

A superb example of Prague Art Nouveau with a beautiful façade and magnificent interior furnishings is the *House of Representation (page 16)*. Prague's citizens call this venue, located next to the *Powder Tower (page 18)*, the *Repre* for short. Architects O. Polívka and A. Balšánek engaged the best Czech artists for the artistic ornamentation. One admires the beautiful decoration in the two restaurants and in the café. From there it is only a short walk to the street called *Na příkopě*, where a trench divided the New and Old Towns in the Middle Ages, and today the pretty *Art Nouveau house at number 7* attracts one's attention. Additional Art Nouveau buildings worth seeing include the *Palais Koruna (at 1 Wenceslas Square)* and the *Hotel Ambassador (at 5 Wenceslas Square)*.

Somewhat further at *No. 29*, one should not miss the *Hotel Evropa* and its interior. The two-storey oval café, with its original interior, lamps, furniture, and inlaid wood railings, form the heart of the building. The so-called *Peterka House (at 12 Wenceslas Square)*, built in 1900 by the 28-year-old star architect of Czech Modernism, Jan Kotěra, produced an especially stylistically pure Art Nouveau building for Prague. The *Palais Lucerna*, a gigantic block with two arcades *(entrances at 38 Wenceslas Square and at 36 Vodičkova)*, accommodates, among other things, a cinema. There is a memorial bust of the architect of the complex, the grandfather of President Václav Havel. In the former *department store, Novák (30 Vodičkova)*, are collected all of the elements of Art Nouveau. Especially impressive is the finely coloured *mosaic* from Jan Preisler on the façade. In the street known as *Národní*, one finds difficulty in deciding which of the two neighbouring Art Nouveau houses has the most beautiful façade: the *Topič House (No. 7)* or the *former Savings and Loan (No. 9)*. Behind the National Theatre, on the banks of the Vltava, the *Masarykovo nábřeží*, there are several Art Nouveau buildings, the *German Goethe Institute (No. 32)* and the house *No. 16* being the most noticeable. From here one can make a detour to the *main railway station* in the Wilsonova, which is distinguished by a remarkable and spacious ticket hall. Or one continues the walk along the Vltava toward *Pařížská*, a street containing several town houses in the Art Nouveau style. Across the *Čech Bridge (page 19)*, which is also built in the Art Nouveau style, we come to the *Letná Park*. The amusing cast-iron *Hanau Pavilion* from 1891, with some Art Nouveau elements, houses a restaurant and a café today. Not far away, at *1 Mickiewiczova (page 41)*, the sculptor František Bílek built a house of his own design, 'to pay homage to Art Nouveau'. The walk ends there.

The gardens (zahradas) on Petřín Hill, once belonged to the residences of the aristocracy and the monasteries, their beauty can be admired today on a two-hour walk.

The starting point for this walk in the spacious park, comprising several gardens, is the tram stop *Újezd (trams 6, 9, 12 and 22)*. From there a cable car ascends *Petřín* Hill – its name derives from the Latin *petra*

(rock). During the day one sees families with children, in the evening lovers use the park for lengthy strolls. The intermediate stop on the distance covered by the *cable car (daily 9.15 am– 8.45 pm)*, a former wine estate, is the *Restaurant Nebozízek* today. We get off at the terminus near one of the lovely ☙ *vista paths* leading through the Strahov Garden. We pass the Gothic *Hunger Wall* from the year 1360, which was once a part of the city fortifications. According to legend, Emperor Charles IV built it to create work for the starving Bohemian people. From the little *Eiffel Tower*, with its 299 steps, and which was planned and built in 1891 within five months, one has a grand view ☙ of the city. With the tower, is an attraction for young and old, a *pavilion with a mirrored cabinet, mirror labyrinth, and a diorama*. This diorama, a gigantic three-dimensional model, shows the battle of the Prague students with the Swedes on the Charles Bridge in 1648. Nearby is the small *Church of St Laurentius*. A passage through the Hunger Wall leads into the *Růžový sad* (rose garden) and to the *Public Observatory*. There are several paths to stroll on here: back to the cable car; on the vista path to *Strahov Monastery (page 46)*; or down to the street called *Vlašská*, past the *German Embassy (page 25)* to the Little Quarter Ring. Another possibility for a lovely walk is the path to *Strahov Stadium*, which holds an audience of 220,000 and where rock and pop concerts take place today.

③ A VIEW OF BAROQUE PRAGUE

Along the Royal Bohemian Coronation Procession one walks to the Castle in four hours from the centre of the city past many interesting sights.

In May, 1743, all of the bells in Prague were rung. Her Royal and Imperial Majesty was greeted with cheers of 'Vivat Maria Theresia!' In an enclosed coach she drove on the Royal Bohemian Coronation Procession, through the festively decorated Old Town and the Little Quarter, to the Castle.

As Maria Theresia did, we emerge from the street known as *Na příkopě* through the *Powder Tower (page 18)* into the crooked lanes of the Old Town. The *Celetná* is lined almost exclusively with Baroque houses which bear *old house names* or *ancient house signs*. At *No. 34* is the superior Cubist house, *The Black Madonna (page 42)*.

Only a few steps ahead of us opens the Market Square – laid out in the 9th century – of the *Old Town Ring,* dominated by the towers of *Týn Church (page 24)*. To save space within the city walls, the sumptuous Gothic town houses were built both narrow and small. The greatest attraction on the Square is the *Astronomical Clock (page 18)*: On every full hour the 12 apostels march past astonished visitors. The triangular *Little Ring* is surrounded by Baroque buildings and medieval arbours. In the richly painted *Rott House* there is a delicatessen where one can find some welcome refreshments for the walk to come.

The royal coach continued the drive, over 250 years ago, through the lane called *Karlova*. The majestic *Old Town Bridge Tower (page 17)* is actually the Arc de Triomphe of the Coronation Procession and the loveliest medieval bridge tower in Europe. The seated figures of Charles IV and his son Václav IV look down from there.

The foundation stone of the *Charles Bridge (page 19)* was laid by Charles IV on July 9th, 1357 at 5.31 am, as the unfavourable influence of Saturn was overcome by the Sun – according to the astrologers of the day, it was most suitable moment of the year. The magic of uneven numbers played an important role; the date as such presented a symmetrically rising and falling series: 135797531. The most popular figure among the thirty sumptuous Baroque groups of statues lining the bridge, is the *Turk (page 19)* in the 14th group of *St John of Matha* on the left side of the bridge; he is the personification of the terror of the Turkish Wars in Europe. Souvenir hunters robbed him recently of his sabre. It was not the first it had happened: the 'flying reporter' Egon Erwin Kisch had already published in his book *Prague Pitaval* the delightful story of 'how the Turk on the Charles Bridge lost his sabre'. (Don't just keep an eye on your sabre here, but on your camera and wallet, too!) At the end of the 16th century the imperial feather trimmer purchased the house *Of the Three Ostriches (at the end of the bridge on the right)* and decorated the building with a fresco depicting three ostriches. At the house restaurant dined famous personalities such as Barbra Streisand and the director of the well-known film *Amadeus,* Miloš Forman.

The royal coach left the Charles Bridge and drove through the Little Quarter – passing numerous *palaces of the aristocracy,* of which some serve as embassies today. The wide *Mostecká* (Bridge Lane) is dominated by the enormous green dome of the Baroque *Church of St Niklas (page 23).* On the Little Quarter side of the Charles Bridge one still finds *tourist-free zones in the picturesque lanes, or in the little squares* on both sides of the bridge. To the left one passes through the *Lázeňská* lane to the Order of the Maltese Knights and their church *Maria Chain* (1169). Here at *14 Maltézské náměstí,* lived a vicious woman who, according to legend, was known as the *Teufelsbaba* (the Devil's Grandmother). The little river, *Čertovka* (Devil's Stream) is named after her. As one turns to the right into the *Míšeňská,* one enters *Vojanovy Park* which contains three chapels founded by the nuns of the Monastery of the Barefoot Carmelites in 1680.

The royal coach circles the *Little Quarter Ring* that served the people of Prague as early as 966 as a market square: It then turned into the steep *Nerudova.* This Little Quarter road is lined with town houses, each with its ancient name. Fifty-two of them also have *picturesque house signs.* The most beautiful is called *The Three Violins (No. 12)* and shows the sign of no less than three generations of violin makers. There is a small restaurant in the house as well, and an anecdote tells of the cook playing the violin as he worked – in a minor key, mind you, to make the meat tender.

Jan Neruda the poet, was born in *The House of the Two Suns,* after which the Nerudova is named. The aristocratic palaces here show their pompous exteriors, as at *No. 5,* where two Moors support the balcony of *Morzin Palace (page 26).* Two heraldic coats of arms of the famous Baroque sculptor Matthias Braun guard the entrance of the *Italian Embassy (No. 20).*

The last part of the Coronation Procession led Maria Theresia's coach across the wide *Hradschin Square (page 30)* with its magnificent palaces. The square enters the *Castle Ramp* to the right; from there the new 16th-century Castle stairway leads to the Little Quarter. One enjoys here a unique ✂ view of the city: Behind the colourful roofs of the Little Quarter labyrinth winds the Vltava, and dozens of towers, large and small, rise on the skyline of the Old and New Towns. One learns why Prague is also lovingly known as the *Little Mother of a Hundred Towers.* The royal coach, however, went on through the Castle portal, which is dominated by the two *Battling Giants* created by Ignác Platzer, and came to a halt in the Courtyard of Honour. The Lord of the Castle greeted Maria Theresia in Czech, she answered him in German. To fanfares and drum beats she continued her Procession to the grandest sight in all the land – *Prague Castle (page 30).*

Practical information

*Useful addresses, information and survival tips
alphabetically listed for quick reference*

ACCOMMODATION

Čedok (109/D3)
*Mon–Fri 9 am–16 pm, Sat 9 am–
1 pm; Na příkopě 18, Tel:
24 19 73 53, Fax: 24 22 22 72, Metro: Můstek (A und B)*

Key System (107/D2)
This is an international agency
which helps you book accom-
modation (also at short notice) in
Prague and in the entire Czech
Republic. *Slezská ulice 13, Mon–
Fri 8 am–5 pm; Tel: 21 00 15 40,
Fax: 21 00 15 44, e-mail address:
keypr@mailserv.bohem-net.cz.*

Prague Tourist Center (108/C3)
*Daily 9 am–6 pm; Rytířská 12,
Tel and Fax: 24 21 22 09, Metro:
Můstek (A and B)*

BANKS & MONEY

The Czech unit of currency is
the crown (*koruna – Kč*) which is
divided into 100 heller (*haléř*).
Bank notes come in denom-
inations of 20, 50, 100, 200, 500,
1000, 2000 and 5000 Kč. Only
the bigger hotels, shops and
restaurants will credit cards.

The normal opening hours for
banks are from 9 am to 12 am and
from 1 pm to 4 pm. The majority of banks and bureaux de
change are concentrated on and
around Wenceslas Square and on
Na příkope. It's worth noting that
banks charge a commission of
1–3 percent for each transaction,
while the bureaux de change
commission charges can be any-
thing between 4 and 9 percent.

CUSTOMS

Souvenirs and gifts can be
exported duty-free. Objets d'art
and antiques, however, can only
be exported with the official
permission of the Czech author-
ities. Additional information can
be obtained from the *Customs
Office; Wenceslas Square 24;
Tel: 24 22 61 17.* Every customs
office provides a list of all the
items for which exportation is
prohibited; needless to say, these
regulations should be followed
to the letter.

There is a new regulation recently introduced stipulating that
all visitors to the Czech Republic
must carry at least 500 Kč per day
in cash or the equivalent in
foreign currency. This law is
being implemented to reduce the
numbers of illegal workers.

DRIVING

The speed limits are: 50 km/h in urban areas; elsewhere 90 km/h, 130 km/h on the motorway.
Breakdown service: UAMK, Tel: 123 (outside Prague: 0123); ABA, Tel: 124; Info: Tel: 61 10 43 33.

EMBASSIES

Britain (101/E5)
Thunovská 14, Malá Strana
Tel: 24 51 05 32
Metro: Malostranská (A)

Canada (101/E5)
Mickwiczova 6, Prague 6
Tel: 24 31 11 08
Metro: Hradčanská

USA (101/E5)
Tržiště 15, Malá Strana
Tel: 24 51 08 47
Metro: Malostranská (A)

EMERGENCIES

Ambulance – Tel: 155
Breakdown – Tel: 123
Police – Tel: 158 (free)

FOREIGN LANGUAGE GUIDES

If you want a more in depth understanding of the country's historical background and cultural riches, it is a good idea to hire a foreign language guide, particu-larly when visiting the Royal Castle and the Jewish Museum.

Prague Castle (101/E5)
Second courtyard (Chapel of the Holy Cross); Tel: 24 37 33 68

Jewish Museum (108/C1)
U starého hřbitova 3A, Tel: 231 03 02 and 2 31 71 91

GEOGRAPHY

Area: 497 sq km (192 sq mi). Inhabitants: 1.2 million (1996). Latitude: 50° North, Longitude: 14° East. Average altitude: 235m (750ft). Climate: average temperature in July 19.2°C (67°F); in January 0°C (32°F). Vltava: length in Prague, 31km (50mi); average depth, 3–4m (10-12ft); greatest width, 330m (1000ft). 10 islands, 18 bridges, approx. 500 towers.

GUIDED TOURS

There are over a dozen offering sightseeing tours companies in the city centre. Recommended: the *Ekoexpres*, a kind of small train which goes from the Old Town Ring to the Castle and back, passing the major tourist attractions along the way. With commentary in six different languages. Guided walks are also quite popular. Information at the PIS-Info bureaus.

LISTINGS

Monthly programmes listing all cultural events in Prague and other helpful brochures can be picked up in the Old Town Hall and in all PIS-Infos: *Prague Cultural Events, Prague Travel Guide* and *Welcome to Prague.*

MEDICAL ASSISTANCE

Doctor: Tel: 2 42 22 52 01, Mon–Fri 7 pm–7 am, all day Sat and Sun; Dentist: Tel: 24 21 60 32, Mon–Fri 7 pm–7 am, all day Sat and Sun. The address for both: Palackého 5 (**109/D4**)

PETROL/GASOLINE

The number of service stations along the main routes is increasing all the time. Unleaded petrol (95 octane) is known as *Natural.*

Service stations open 24 hours:
Žižkov, Olšanská (**107/F1**); *Smíchov, Plzeňská* (**104/A3**); *Holešovice, Argentinská* (**103/D3**); *Žižkov, Kališnická* (**103/F5**)

PHARMACIES

Lékárna
The pharmacies at Štefánikova 6, Metro: Anděl (B) (**105/E3**), *and Belgická 37, Metro: Náměstí Míru (C)* (**106/C2**) *are open around the clock every day of the week*

POST OFFICES & TELEPHONE

Post offices (*Pošta*) are easily identified by their large orange sign. The main post office at *Jindřišská 14* is open 24 hours a day. Stamps for letters (20g) to all European countries cost 8 Kč, postcards are 6 Kč, letters to destinations outside Europe are 11 Kč, postcards 7 Kč.

Ask your guide to take you to the Belvedere, a remarkable Renaissance palace

If you want to phone abroad, dial the country code first (0044 for the UK, 00353 for Ireland, and 001 for Canada and the USA), followed by the local number omitting the zero prefix. International prefix for calls to the Czech Republic: 0042 (Prague: 00422). Local calls cost 2 Kč and telephone cards (valid for national and international calls) are available from post offices and newsagents.

Pronunciation of the Czech language is not easy, but the following guidelines should at least help you to read some of the street names and menu items:

The accented vowels á, é, í, ó, ú are all long; the consonant č is pronounced 'ch' as in 'church', while c sounds like ts; h is always pronounced; j sounds like y; ň is like the 'ni' in 'onion'; š sounds like the 'sh' in 'ship'; ř sounds like r and ž combined; ž sounds like the 's' in pleasure.

PUBLIC TRANSPORT

The Metro is the fastest means of transport and has three lines: Line A is green, B is yellow, C is red. Náměstí míru (A) is the station built deepest into the ground at 52m (160 ft). A transfer ticket for the metro, trams and buses costs 12 Kč, children between the ages of 6 and 15 years pay half fare; children under 6 years of age ride free. The ticket offers unlimited transfers and is valid for one hour (90 minutes on weekends, public holidays and between 8 pm and 5 am. Also available are

short-trip tickets (no transfers), valid for a 15 minute ride on trams or busses or for 4 stops on the metro; it costs 8 Kč (children between the ages of 6 and 15 again pay half fare. Network tickets (valid 1, 3, 7 or 15 days) cost 60–250 Kč. Some useful terms for the metro: *směr* (direction); *výstup* (exit); *přestup* (transfer). The metro runs from 5 am to midnight. Tickets are on sale at newsstands, in tobacco shops or from the vending machines in the metro stations.

TAXI

The basic charge is 20–30 Kč, then 16–18 Kč per km. It is best to order a taxi by calling the *AAA* dispatching centre, *Tel: 10 80.* Just to be on the safe side, inquire about the fare before boarding!

THEATRE TICKETS

Theatre and concert tickets can be purchased at any of the larger hotels. Also at ticket agencies:

BTI – Bohemia (109/D3)
Mon–Fri 9 am–6 pm, Sat 9 am–4 pm, Sun 10 am–3 pm; Na příkopě 16, Tel: 24 21 50 31, Metro: Náměstí Republiky (B)

Ticketpro (108/C2)
Mon–Fri 8 am–8 pm, Sat 9 am–8 pm, Sun 12 am–8 pm; Salvátorská 10, Tel: 24 81 60 20, Metro: Staroměstská (A)

TICKETS (INTERNAL FLIGHTS)

Čedok (109/D3)
Na příkopě 18, Mon–Fri 8.30 am–6 pm, Sat 9 am–2 pm; Metro: Můstek (A and B)

TIPPING

It is customary to tip waiters in both cafés and restaurants, as well as taxi drivers, guides, porters, chamber maids and hotel staff. If you make a table reservation, a small tip is also recommended.

TOILETS

Toilets (WC) are marked *Dámy* or *Ženy* for women and *Páni* or *Muži* for men.

TOURIST INFORMATION

The Prague Information Service (PIS) runs several PIS-Info bureaus which provide tourist and accommodation information and also sell maps and theatre tickets. Office locations:
Na příkopě 20, Metro: Můstek (A and B) (**109/D3**); *Old Town Hall, Staroměstské náměstí, Metro: Staroměstská (A)* (**108/C2**); *Central Railway Station, Metro: Hlavní nádraží (C)* (**109/F3-4**); *Bridge Tower (Little Quarter), Metro: Malostranská (A)* (**108/A2**)

VISAS

In order to enter the Czech Republic, all British, Irish, American and most EU nationals require only a valid passport, but Canadians as well as Australian nationals need to obtain a visa (which is usually valid for 30 days).

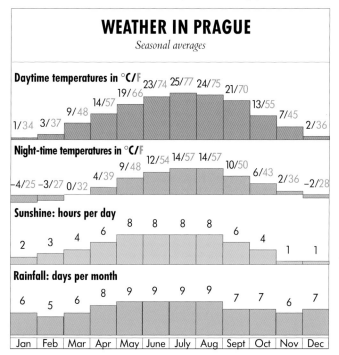

WEATHER IN PRAGUE
Seasonal averages

Daytime temperatures in °C/F

1/34 3/37 9/48 14/57 19/66 23/74 25/77 24/75 21/70 13/55 7/45 2/36

Night-time temperatures in °C/F

-4/25 -3/27 0/32 4/39 9/48 12/54 14/57 14/57 10/50 6/43 2/36 -2/28

Sunshine: hours per day

2 3 4 6 8 8 8 8 6 4 1 1

Rainfall: days per month

6 5 6 8 9 9 9 9 7 7 6 7

| Jan | Feb | Mar | Apr | May | June | July | Aug | Sept | Oct | Nov | Dec |

Do's and don'ts

*Some tips on how to avoid the traps and pitfalls
the unwary traveller may fall into*

Driving offences
Given the absolute ban on drinking and driving, avoid all alcoholic beverages (even beer) if you plan to get behind the wheel. What's more, the fine has been increased to 15 'Palackýs' (this is a 1000 Kč note named after historian Frantisek Palacks, whose picture appears on it). Speeding will cost you two 'Palackýs'.

Minor thieves
Children specialised in stealing have recently been smuggled over the border from south-east Europe. They operate where many tourists are concentrated in small areas. Their companions are also disguised as tourists. The police are powerless because the children are not of the age of criminal responsibility. Don't panic: but watching out is better than losing out!

Parking
There are several public car parks in the city centre. The main ones are under the National Theatre, at the Rudolfinum and next to the State Opera. If you park illegally, your car will most certainly be towed away. Either that, or you will be clamped and forced to pay a heavy fine.

There are several public parking areas in the city, as well as parking blocks.

Money changers
You should change your money either at the border, or in hotels, bureaux de change or banks. Banks charge a commission fee of 1 to 3 percent, while the private bureaux de change charge 4 to 9 percent. You should avoid the money changers on the streets, as they often distribute counterfeit notes.

Taxi drivers
According to legislation by the Prague Town Hall, all taxis must operate with a meter. A great deal of swindling takes place. One must also ensure that the meter indicator is properly set!

A passion for car stealing
There are a number of international car thief gangs in Prague whose favourite targets are Volkswagen Golfs and Audis. Always make sure your car is secure or it will quickly disappear to the East.

White clothing
The change-over to oil-burning power-generating stations is progressing slowly but coal, which does significantly pollute the atmosphere, is still widely used for fuel. It might therefore be a good idea to avoid wearing white clothes when you are walking around Prague.

Street Atlas of Prague

*Please refer to back cover for an overview
of this street atlas*

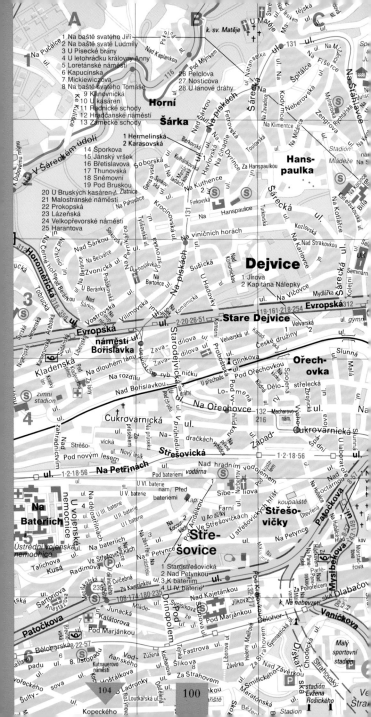

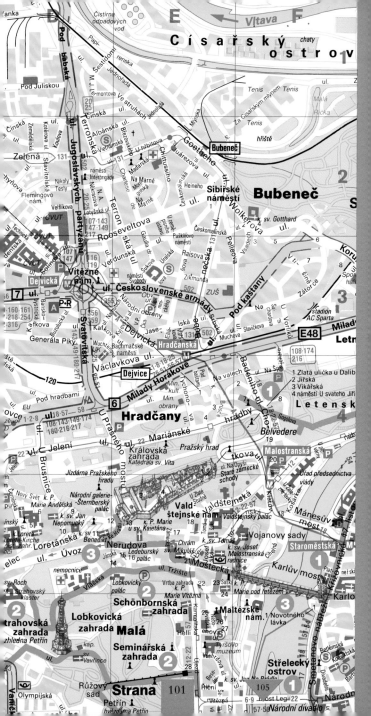

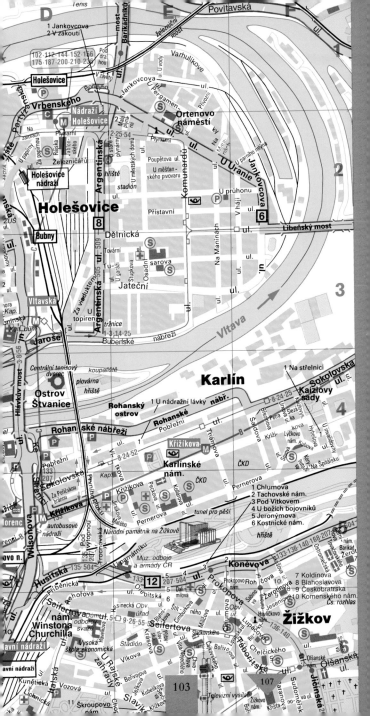

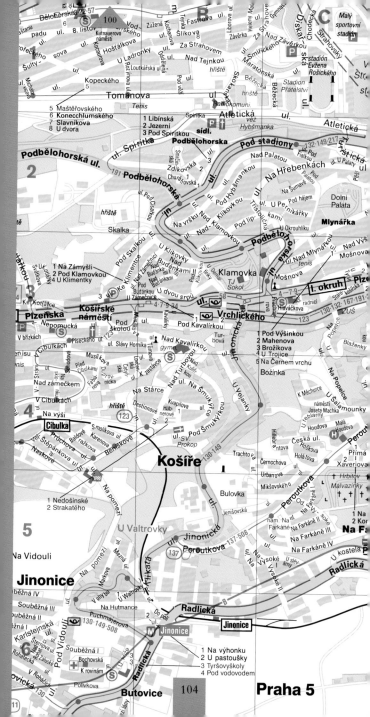

Praha 5

zahrada
ledna Petřín

Seminářská
zahrada

Strana

Růžový
sad

Petřín
hvězdárna Petřín

Kinského zahrada

Olympijská

Chaloupeckého

Jezdecká
Sermíská

103-176

ebenká

U Nesyp
Švédská

Grafická

Duškova

sovy sady

U Věnečku

Mrázovka

Fráni Šrámka

U Blaženky

Mrázovka

Filip
a Jakub
Štorkánova

icá

Radlice

SPŠ Helli
grafická

Tyršovo
muzeum

Střelecký
ostrov

101

k. sv. Jan Na Prádle

most Legií 22

Národní divadlo

Dětský
ostrov

Slovanský
ostrov

1 V lesíčku
2 Arbesovo namesti

Myslík

Ressl

Jiráskův most

1 nám. 14. října
2 Preslova
3 Pecháková
Lesnická

Palackého
most

Bazilika
sv. Václava

Matoušova

Na bělidle

Anděl

Vltavská

Ostrov
ského

Za Ženskými
domovy

Smíchov

5 Palackého
náměstí
6 náměstí Pod
Emauzy
7 Dřevěná
8 Na pořičním
právu
9 Na Děkance

U železničního
mostu

Sady
Na skalce

103

Smíchovské nádraží

přístav

Smíchov

Kesnerka

Radlická

U starého židovského
hřbitova

Pod Kesnerkou

Pod Kesnerkou

tenis

Radlice

vodárna

Císařská
louka

Vodácký
stadión

Vesl
ost

1 Nad sokolovnou
2 U podolského hřbitov
3 Na Kavčích horách

SK.
Smíchov Praha

105

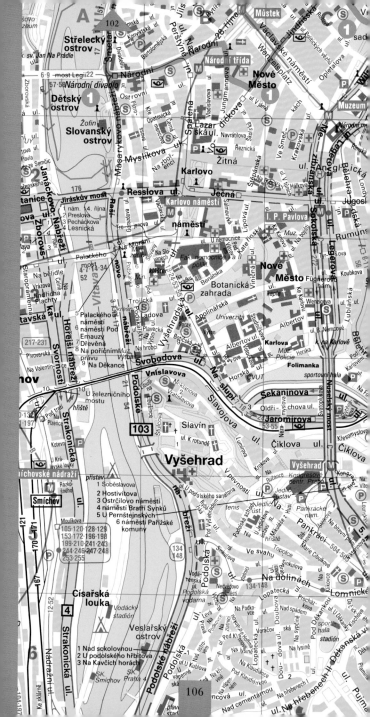

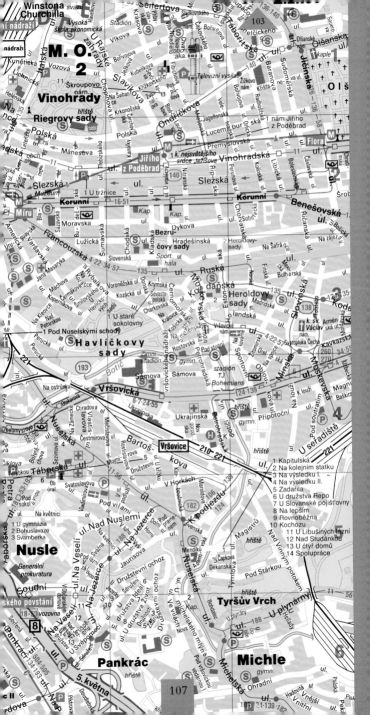

Cityplan

1 : 10 500

200 m
400 ft

A

Dražického nám.

Vojanovy sady

1 U lužického semináře

Míšeňská

Saská

Cihelná

1 Dražického

Karlův most

Lichtenštejnský palác

Hroznová

Na Kampě

Kampa

Čertovka

U Sovových mlýnů

Sovovy mlýny

U lužického semináře

3

Vltava

Střelecký ostrov

Muzeum B. Smetany

Novotného lávka

Říční ul.

Ma-lostranské nábř.

1 Všehrdova

4

Vítězná

Zborovská

Janáčkovo

Petřínská ul.

most Legií 6·9·22·51

Akademie múzických umění

Dětský ostrov

5

Vodní ul.

Malátova ul.

ul. Pavla Švandy ze Semčic

nábřeží

6

Kořenského nábřeží

ul. V botanice

Dienzenhoferovy sady

Matoušova ul.

176 **Jiráskův most**

B

Alšovo

Vysoká škola umělecko-průmyslová

Dvořákovo

Jana Palacha nám.

Křižovnická

k. sv. František Platnéřská
z Assisi

Klementinum

k. Karel IV

k. sv. Salvátor

Karlova

Křižovnické nám.

Anenské nám. Na zábradlí Anenská

Betlémská kaple

Náprstkova ul.

Boršov

Betlémské Náprstkovo nám.
muz.

Betlémská

Střední průmyslová ská ul.
škola strojnická

Konviktská

kaple

Divadelní

Smetanovo nábř.

Krocínova ul.

Národní divadlo

Národní

Divadelní

Klášter sester voršilek

k. sv. Voršila

Ostrovní

Masarykovo

Slovanský ostrov

ul. Na struze

Šítkovská

k. sv. Vojtěch

Vojtěšská

Petrossova

Opatovická

Voršilská

Na Perštýně

Bartoloměnská

Křemencova

V Jirchářích

Na struze

Černá

Myslíkova

Na Zderaze

Záhořanského ul.

Náplavní

Jiráskovo nám. **Resslova**

k. sv. Cyril a Metoděj

Trojická

Jenštejnská

Gorazdova

C

Simon a Juda

Pařížská

Curie-ových nám.

Universita Karlova

Filharmonie

Na rejdišti

Rudolfinum

Umělecko-průmyslové muzeum

Široká

Veleslavínova

Mariánské nám.

Magistrát

Linhartská

nám. Jana Palacha

Bílkova

Staronová synagoga

Klausova synagoga

Pinkasova synagoga

Maiselova syn.

Žid. Muz.

Kaprova ul.

Mariánské nám.

k. sv. Jiljí

Jilská

Michalská

Zlatá

k. sv. Michal

Lazarská

Karlovo nám.

Staroměstská

Maiselova

Jáchymova

k. sv. Mikuláš

Malé nám.

Hlavsova

Vejvodova

Skořepka

Uhelný trh

Martinská

k. sv. Martin

Národní třída

Spálená

Purkyňova ul.

Novoměstská Prokuratura a soudy

Odborů

Na zbořenci

Vodičkova

Jungmannovo nám.

Melantrichova

Havelská

Václavské nám.

Kostelní kap.

k. sv. Václav 176

Hřbitova

Karlovo nám.

108

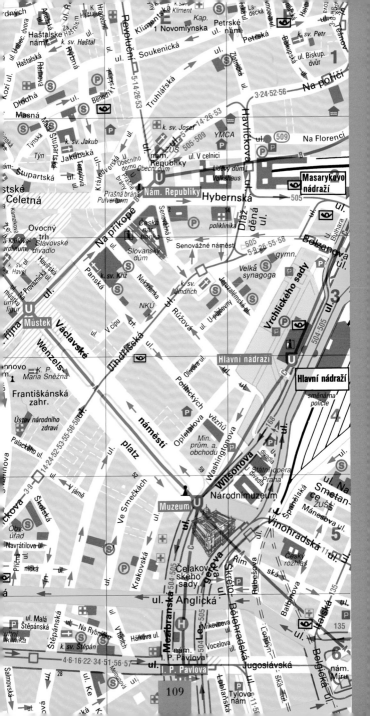

109

STREET ATLAS LEGEND

Symbol	German	English
	Autobahn mit Nummer	Motorway with number
	Schnellstraße/Bundesstraße	Motor highway/Federal road
	Hauptstraße	Mainroad
	Übrige Straßen/Weg	Other roads/Footpath
	Straßen in Bau/Planung	Roads under construction/projected
	Fußgängerzone/Einbahnstraße	Pedestrian zone/One-way street
	Eisenbahn mit Bahnhof	Railway with station
	Güter- und Industriebahn	Freight and industrial railway
U7 U6 / M	U-Bahn/Stadtbahn	Underground/Light Rail
698 / 641	Bus/Straßenbahn mit Endhaltestelle	Bus/Tramway with terminus
	Fähre	Ferry
	Wald/Park	Forest/Park
+++	Friedhof, Weinberg	Cemetery, Vineyard

Symbol	German	English
i	Tourist-Information	Tourist information centre
⊞ Ⓢ Ⓔ	Krankenhaus/Schule	Hospital/School
Ⓕ Ⓟ	Feuerwehr/Polizei	Fire station/Police station
	Campingplatz/Jugendherberge	Camping site/Youth hostel
◁◁	Post	Post office
	Försterei	Forester's lodge
	Einzelne Bäume	Isolated trees
	Sendeanlage/Leuchtturm	Transmitting station/Lighthouse
	Denkmal/Mühle/Windmühle	Monument/Mill/Windmill
K B C E C A	Konsulat/Botschaft	Consulate/Embassy
P P	Parkplatz/Parkhaus/Tiefgarage	Car park/Parking house/Underground car park
	Hallenbad	Indoor swimming pool

500 m
1000 ft

Marco Polo Walking Tours

1 Art Nouveau Buildings Along the Vltava

2 Idyllic Gardens in the City Centre

3 A View of Baroque Prague

This index lists a selection of the streets and squares shown in the street atlas

114

This index lists all the main sights, museums, restaurants and hotels mentioned in this guide.

What do you get for your money?

Rates of exchange differ from day to day – check the newspapers for current exchange rates. Despite the recent high inflation, many goods and services offered in Prague are still relatively cheap compared with Western Europe. The currency of the Czech Republic is the Czech crown – koruna česká. The official exchange rate of the crown (Kč) is reasonably stable. Hotel prices are not regulated, and during the summer and peak periods, such as Easter and Whitsun, they can rise sharply. Private accommodation and rooms in guesthouses provide cheap options to the hotels with prices averaging between 400 and 600 Kč per person per day. If you wish to venture further out, excursions to some of the beautiful chateaux in the surrounding areas of Prague – the imperial palace at Karlstejn or the ducal palace at Konopiste for example – can be quite cheap. One-day or half-day excursions to the castles of southern Bohemia, or the cosmopolitan town of Karlovy Vary, even boat trips down the Vltava can all be enjoyed for a reasonable price. Here are a few sample prices to give you an idea of what you can get for your money. A single journey on the metro, on a tram or on a bus costs 12 Kč. A bus tour of the city is 400–500 Kč. A standard postcard costs 3–5 Kč , the postage is 6 Kč within Europe and 7 Kč outside Europe (letters cost 8 Kč per 20g). A local telephone call is 2 Kč.

US$	Czech Crown (Kč)	£	Czech Crown (Kč)	Can$	Czech Crown (Kč)
1	30.00	1	50.00	1	20.00
2	60.00	2	100.00	2	40.00
3	90.00	3	150.00	3	60.00
4	120.00	4	200.00	4	80.00
5	150.00	5	250.00	5	100.00
10	200.00	10	500.00	10	200.00
15	300.00	15	750.00	15	300.00
20	400.00	20	1000.00	20	400.00
25	500.00	25	1250.00	25	500.00
30	600.00	30	1500.00	30	600.00
40	800.00	40	2000.00	40	800.00
50	1000.00	50	2500.00	50	1000.00
60	1200.00	60	3000.00	60	1200.00
70	1400.00	70	3500.00	70	1400.00
80	1600.00	80	4000.00	80	1600.00
90	1800.00	90	4500.00	90	1800.00
100	2000.00	100	5000.00	100	2000.00
200	4000.00	200	10000.00	200	4000.00
300	6000.00	300	15000.00	300	6000.00
400	8000.00	400	20000.00	400	8000.00
500	10000.00	500	25000.00	500	10000.00
750	15000.00	750	37500.00	750	15000.00
1000	20000.00	1000	50000.00	1000	20000.00